she

she & me

~

Bhavarlal H. Jain

SHE & ME

Bhavarlal H. Jain, the founder and chairman of Jain Irrigation Systems Ltd, is widely known as the man who changed the lives of millions of Indian farmers through his pioneering work in the field of micro-irrigation. He has written a number of books in Marathi and English. This book was originally published in Marathi as *Ti ani Mi*, and went on to become a bestseller. The book has also been translated into Hindi.

RUPA

Published by
Rupa Publications India Pvt. Ltd 2014
7/16, Ansari Road, Daryaganj
New Delhi 110002

Sales Centres:

Allahabad Bengaluru Chennai
Hyderabad Jaipur Kathmandu
Kolkata Mumbai

Copyright © Bhavarlal H. Jain 2014

All rights reserved.
No part of this publication may be reproduced, transmitted,
or stored in a retrieval system, in any form or by any means,
electronic, mechanical, photocopying, recording or otherwise,
without the prior permission of the publisher.

ISBN: 978-81-291-3565-0

First impression 2014

10 9 8 7 6 5 4 3 2 1

The moral right of the author has been asserted.

Printed at Parksons Graphics Pvt. Ltd, Mumbai

This book is sold subject to the condition that it shall not,
by way of trade or otherwise, be lent, resold, hired out, or otherwise
circulated, without the publisher's prior consent, in any form of binding or
cover other than that in which it is published.

*This is an unusual but real,
autobiographical heart-to-heart talk.*

*Whichever couple likes it and decides to emulate it,
would live happily ever after!*

Dedicating with this trust.

She...

HER INFECTIOUS LAUGHTER. The way she talked, her fleeting glances, the effortless way she worked...these lingering memories occupy a special place in my heart even today and surface time and again, making my heart feel like a garden. When she was with me, she was practically invisible. Now that she is no more, her presence pervades my every waking moment. And I know, this is how it will be, for as long as I live; and it will keep my memories of four decades of togetherness fresh and unfading.

The need to tell this story arises from the prevailing thought among many self-centred modern couples that bearing children is not the primary purpose of marriage; it is, in fact, best avoided. This thought has gained fashionable acceptance in the minds of the young generation. They maintain that if at all they are to raise children, one or two would be just about okay. More children would mean an extra burden. Life would become a drudgery, an endless round of chores and responsibilities from changing nappies to fetching them from school. If one had to deal with the nitty-gritties of child rearing, what was the point of being highly educated with several degrees in the first place! If we are to execute the chores that can be performed by baby-sitters and maids, then what would be the difference between them and us? Besides, we also have to pay attention to our personal grooming, to look presentable; after all these things matter a lot today if one is to advance one's career. And anyway, for whom are we doing all this? Not just for ourselves, but for the good of the whole family. In these selfish times, no friend or relative will stand by us in our hour of need. It is better to be self-sufficient. In today's world, it is the language of money that matters, and if we don't have money, where do we stand in society? Relatives and friends will desert us at the slightest hint of trouble. What will be our plight then? We have to take charge of our future without depending on anyone. A decent life and a decent bank balance will more than compensate for the adjustments that we will have to make as a working couple. If we achieve work stability and financial security, the rest will automatically fall into place. People will respect us, and we will be able to live in comfort and luxury. This is what will make life worthwhile.

A young woman might think: 'My generation was never brought up to be a housewife. With my lifestyle and education, I cannot be tied down to the kitchen. All the restaurants and hotels and multiplexes and malls in town would go out of business if modern women were to live aimless, restricted lives, confined to their homes. There is a whole world of opportunities and enjoyment beyond the loathsome kitchen, and I belong to that world. If I am tired after work or not in the mood to cook some evenings, what are "instant mixes" for? Or better still, we can go out with friends and have a decent meal.'

Leisure is created in today's hectic times by reducing the workload at home. And that spare time is used in activities like non-stop TV watching, going for multiple movies in multiplexes, and what is generally called having a good time. And as far as the baby is concerned, there are those mushrooming nanny services and even those professionally qualified baby-sitters. The fact that they will not only take care of the baby, but will also groom it during its formative years is completely overlooked. And as soon as the children are of school-going age, another option is available (for today's professionals): a professionally managed, socially upbeat and expensive boarding school. So that takes care of the children's upbringing in the best possible manner. And so responsibilities are passed on.

With time for ourselves, we have some scope for our personal development. We can enjoy our free time. Just SMS the caterer, and that delicious dinner or that piping hot pizza is home-delivered within no time. They even give a money-back guarantee if an oven-fresh pizza is not delivered within 30 minutes of ordering it! So, why slog and sweat when ready-made items are instantly available?

Today's couples need their 'space', and they are willing to get it by any means and at any cost. They tie the knot only after reaching a clear understanding about how they are going to 'respect' each other's personal space after marriage. After all, they have their own likes and dislikes, preferences and priorities, and these need not be totally compromised just because of marriage. Such 'practical' issues are settled even before the seven sacred vows are taken.

This is what 'space' means to couples today. But the problem begins when the space for 'space' is reduced. For young couples, this 'space' means that they should get some scope and time for their personal, independent pursuits, away from matrimonial life. Space could also mean independence of thought, or simply some time to relax and unwind.

But, how far is all this necessary? Or is it necessary at all?

When two souls and bodies become one in its truest and deepest sense, when there remains nothing which is exclusively 'mine' or 'yours', when both the independent counterparts willingly agree to blend in order to create a monolithic interdependent whole, when both partners unconditionally consent to share everything that the present and the future holds for them, when 'I' and 'mine' merge into one another and become 'we' and 'ours', what relevance does this understanding of independent 'space' have in married life? However, such thinking would appeal to only those couples who are wedded in body, heart and soul, and have earnestly adopted the solemn vow of: 'Until death do us part'. The very idea of independent existence, nay, the very idea of independent life detached from sacred togetherness is absurd for them.

Birth, marriage and death—the three critical events in human life. Of these, the first and the third are not in our hands, but the second one certainly is. Each one of us gets to choose our life-companion, who will not only nurture our future life together, but will also give birth to and nurture our future generation. The selection of our life partners is momentous for all of us, which is solemnized by the seven sacred vows. A marriage thus takes place, binds two souls together and plants the seed of the procreation of our universe. In fact, this whole world is a universal family whose evolution also begins in every family. It is entirely up to us as to how we transform it into a happy, ideal family. We can enact ideal domesticity on the stage that is our family or we can convert it into a conflict zone where we are in a permanent state of disagreement and friction with each other. Good, positive and auspicious thoughts are merely an outward expression of our inner feelings. Paths are made so that one can walk; one does not have to walk merely because paths exist. Those who walk, merely cover the distance; but it is only those who walk with restraint and sagacity, who can reach the destination.

Many couples who walk on the path of life aimlessly just travel the distance, arriving nowhere and achieving nothing at the end of it. But those couples who have common lofty motives, and who walk hand in hand with discipline and restraint, do succeed in creating an idyllic married life. And when does this happen? It certainly cannot happen when life's voyage is reduced to a frenzied race for material comforts. Such a race will inevitably end up in a ruinous marriage—money can acquire only objects of pleasure, not happiness. Couples cannot buy a blissful marriage. It has to be earned by cultivating commonness of purpose and agreement of thoughts. Any great relationship, including marriage, is about two main things. The first is to discover the similarities and the second is to respect the differences. In that sense, married life is a journey of thoughts, ideas and adjustments as much as it is a journey in time.

The strong foundation of the Indian marriage system is based on time-tested practices. The earnest interaction of ideas, the disclosure of expectations and aspirations, the attempt to gauge the compatibility on various parameters, the revelation of each other's future plans, principles and higher objectives—all this is earnestly discussed during the meeting. It does help in making well-informed, balanced decisions. Such prudent customs make Indian marriages strong and 'fail-proof'. Mutual commitment resulting from due consideration of important aspects concerning lifelong compatibility becomes more binding and abiding. It is in this manner that you ultimately discover your inner selves. The positive vibrations felt and the agreement reached with the prospective life partner is almost divine. You meet each other, explore each other's feelings, make each other familiar with your respective ideas about life, the ways to live it and ultimately discover the inner self. This leads to an informed and mature decision that is the basis of the Indian Marriage System.

The next step is to convey the decision to family, friends and near and dear ones. It becomes a bit tricky to talk about such matters to the elders in the family and to obtain their consent–especially from someone like an illiterate mother who is nevertheless astute and pragmatic. However, going through this process and following these time-tested traditions is the personification of one's educational and cultural background. This begins a journey of two unknown souls that will last for generations.

It is believed that your wife bids you her final farewell at the threshold, family and friends carry you to the cremation ground, and your body turns to ashes at the funeral pyre. However, it is one's sins and virtues, thoughts and behaviour that accompany the soul in its onward journey. That is why the cultivation of good thoughts and deeds in life ensures a golden harvest of good karma. People of high moral-ethical stature look to earn these types of rewards from a life, single-mindedly dedicated to upholding a virtuous marriage.

This narrative is an honest and heartfelt effort to sketch the character of just this type of a simple, unassuming and highly virtuous person. She was my wife, my life-companion, my soulmate. The scope of this book also covers the background of our entire Jain family. But then, this family would not have taken root without her nurturing it with utmost love and dedication. Hence, in essence, she is the central character and the moving spirit of this story.

Her name was Kantabai. This is not a book on her, but her book. Only the words are mine. Sometimes, I can't take credit even for the words. She dictated them through fond memories; I was merely the scribe.

I

AS WE PROCEEDED from the Ravivar Karanja area of Nashik (earlier Nasik) towards the railway station in a horse-drawn carriage, my friend Pandhri advised me, 'It is entirely up to you whether you want to make your married life a happy play on life's stage, or make it a battleground.' The context of this dialogue was the promise that I had given to my parents that I would settle down with the right girl as soon as I reached marriageable age, and this visit to Nashik was in pursuit of a marriage proposal. Not being in favour of keeping the girl's family waiting anxiously, I had vowed to myself that I would convey my decision on all matrimonial proposals within a week's time. Also, talks would be expedited where proposals were promising. This Nashik girl's father was a well-known advocate. The girl had inherited the argumentative qualities of her father, and having studied law, I continued the conversation in the same vein. Hence, the whole meeting was farcically converted into a sort of a court hearing! It was because of this that my accompanying friend Pandhrinath Save had expressed his concern whether I wanted to create court scenes in my life after marriage! His candidness compelled me to think further on the matter.

I mischievously said, 'Look Pandhri, will it not be a feather in our cap if our wedding procession, the guests and the entire event, was given a memorable royal treatment by such an affluent family? Will it not boost our reputation instantly?' Pandhri looked at my face quizzically as we travelled in the tanga. The horses' hoofs clip-clopped to a rhythm on the street, and we both were so engrossed in our thoughts that neither knew where we were or where we were going to. He said, 'My friend, these hospitable overtures are all momentary matters. People will soon forget the royal treatment and the lavish gifts.' He was implying that what really mattered was an agreeable and amiable domestic life that starts after marriage and not the pomp and show that ends with the ceremony. I could not have agreed with him more. I said, 'I have my dreams and my set of objectives in life. I am convinced that I will make history. I need a wife who will gladly be with me through the thick and thin of life. One who will unhesitatingly make the sacrifices and face the challenges. One who will always be there for me with a smile or a comforting shoulder. My aims are lofty. My chosen path is an uphill journey, and going forward, I need an "all-weather" partner who sees eye to eye and walks hand in hand with me.'

Pandhri handed in his judgment, 'Then the case is dismissed. This girl, who answered all your queries with counter-queries, and who seemed more concerned about matching your arguments rather than making a good match for you, cannot make the type of life partner you are looking for!'

I laughed at the light-hearted remark but within me, there was turmoil. I had taken it upon myself to select my soulmate. In doing so, I had departed from an unbroken family tradition of generations. I was the only graduate in our large extended family, and thought that higher education should also elevate one's thinking and make it progressive. It should offer one the freedom of a responsible choice.

Although my decision was revolutionary, even rebellious, my illiterate, astute and understanding parents supported it fully. They steadfastly resisted convention and pressure from relatives to stand by me. Thus, the burden of accountability lay with me.

I was truly perplexed by the situation. The courageous and progressive youth in me had chosen to defy the age-old tradition. The underlying thought was: I must ultimately make not only myself, my parents and my family proud, but also society itself. My adventurousness must set an example, not upset a time-tested tradition.

It was thus decided that I would shortlist the proposals that I found favourable and present it to my family. They would then meet those families, after which the matter would be discussed conclusively. Accordingly, I had started meeting prospective brides and their families. I had already visited a traditional and well-to-do family in Tondapur near my native village, Wakod, before coming to Nashik.

The next morning, we were in Bombay (now Mumbai) at my uncle's residence in Ghatkopar. The bell rang, and the guests we were awaiting entered with their daughter. My uncle, Dalubhau welcomed them. I was instantly bowled over by the girl. It was as if her silent charm, dignity and poise had hypnotized me. I lost track of time and place. Till date, I don't remember who had accompanied her; I was totally fascinated by her personality.

She bowed to everyone except me. (I wonder even today, why a wife or in this case a wife-to-be, never bows to her husband?) Her respectful greeting was not a forced formality or pretention. It was almost a natural reflex. It appeared that she had it in her blood to respect everyone. And she was calm and composed, even though this was just her second experience of a matrimonial meeting. Her first, a broken engagement, had left Kantabai shattered. That boy was from abroad and after a brief engagement, had gone back and married some other girl. However, he did show some courtesy by writing a short letter to Kantabai announcing the one-sided break-up. All her dreams were shattered with the stroke of a pen!

In those days, it was considered a comprise to contemplate an alliance with a girl whose engagement had been previously broken. However, her personality, presentability and conduct were compelling enough to invite genuine regard and instant liking. She radiated a natural innocence and compassion. Her dress was simple yet elegant. Her hair was also done up simply and neatly. She came across as simplicity personified! She was a few inches shorter than me, and her weight appeared a few kilos less than mine. A fair complexion; large soft brown eyes; a straight, shapely nose; a few strands of hair falling on her forehead; small ears—overall, she made an attractive picture. A white sari with a lace border, head covered with the pallu, completed the perfect metaphor of a cultured Indian lady that was standing before me.

After a while, everybody left the room on one pretext or the other, giving us a chance to have a personal discussion in an informal atmosphere. It is natural to begin such talks with general topics, so that the initial nervousness is dispelled.

'Your education?'

'BA'

'Oh, you have been to college!'

The answer had come to me as a pleasant surprise. In those days, it was thought neither necessary nor advisable to encourage girls to go in for graduation amongst the Marwadi community. This was particularly true for our Oswal sect. Graduate girls were a rarity, to be found in the most forward and progressive families only.

Kantabai promptly replied, 'No no, I have done my graduation from the SNDT University of Poona (now Pune) through a distance education course.'

'What is your age?'

'I am about to complete 25 years.'

'Good. We are almost the same age—there is hardly a difference of a few months. Same-aged couples are an oddity. Would you mind this?'

'It's not an issue with me if you and your family don't mind.'

'Good, good,' I said, relieving her of her anxiety. I then proceeded, 'As such, considering the burden of household responsibilities, I don't think your education can be put to any purposeful use in our family. Are you career minded?'

'No, I am not particularly interested in doing a job after marriage. Besides, I feel that education can be useful even in homemaking.'

'How is that?' I asked. The advocate in me took over the task of an examiner.

'Education transforms a person's outlook towards work. There is an inherent qualitative difference in the manner in which a given task is accomplished by an educated person and an uneducated person. Our insight, inquiry, observation and intellect get enhanced due to our education and training. Such superior inputs naturally produce better outputs, and this is true even for household chores. I believe that education can be put to good use in many domestic matters, right from hospitality, to maintaining the family and social relations, to bringing up children. Education is what transforms housewives into homemakers.'

'So you sincerely believe that education can improve your standard of life even in non-monetary terms. That it will help you withstand the difficulties and challenges of life in a better and more organized manner?'

'Yes, I do feel that way.'

'But practicality is quite different from this theoretical perception.'

'Excuse me?'

'You will agree that most of the educated women don't think like this nowadays'.

Kantabai remained silent, thus conveying that she was an exception to that general rule. I spoke after a few moments of silence.

'It has become fashionable for educated women to raise the banner of feminism with or without good reason. Disrespect for men seems to be rising along with women's literacy rate. Qualified housewives are taking up careers. They now find core household responsibilities below their "dignity". To feed the family or to respect and look after the elders, even bringing up children seems cumbersome to them. They find it more satisfying and meaningful to work in offices than to manage homes. You do understand what I am saying, don't you?'

Kantabai said, 'Yes, I do. I come across a lot of feminist material in the newspapers and magazines these days. Nevertheless, it is my conviction that a majority of women don't think that way. They find such material neither palatable nor digestible. As I said earlier, education has its due role in the process of homemaking. It is no less a job to raise children properly in a cultured atmosphere. Isn't there a difference between jungle flowers and the ones blooming in a garden?'

'Yes that's very true.' I concluded.

Kantabai continued, 'Looking after the elders in the family is gratitude, not servitude. There is a great deal of inner joy and contentment in serving one's parents-in-law with love and compassion, as if they were one's own parents. I have always felt that God has gifted women with an infinite capacity to love and to care.'

She continued spiritedly, 'Raising children with love, care and concern is also of utmost importance. They are the universe unto themselves, they are our next generation. No career-based reward can match the tremendous pride and privilege that a mother gets from raising worthy children. I fail to understand why women should feel inferior in performing this most admirable task. Besides, I honestly don't think that women are serving their cause any better by competing with men, particularly if they are doing it in utter disregard of their domestic duties.'

Kantabai was simple and candid, yet articulate and convincing. But the lawyer in me could not resist further cross-examining her.

'But it cannot be totally ignored that individuals get a better chance to develop in a small, divided nuclear family. If there is no undue influence on the thought process, individuals can naturally grow in a better way.'

Kantabai was listening to me intently. I continued, 'The elders belong to the previous generation and they have their own ideas which they cannot easily let go of. They cannot forgo the family's sanskaar, the family's cultural footprint, without resistance. These differences will naturally create a generation gap. And given their advanced age and biological factors, the elders are bound to become restive, intolerant, short-tempered and inflexible. Over time, they become irritants to a young couple, who may start finding them old-fashioned and rigid. Their behaviour, their very presence may soon become an oddity and a cause for embarrassment in the family.'

Kantabai nodded in agreement.

I went on, 'I hail from a large extended joint family. It shelters my brother and me, three uncles, and their respective families. It is natural to have diversity of thought, actions, behaviours, attitudes and opinions in such a large family. To live amicably and with dignity in such an environment is not everybody's cup of tea. That is why frictions are created.'

I could read concern on her face, but continued: 'Children are often the root cause of trouble in any family. As it is, we are not wealthy. We are just self-sufficient. Our family cannot be bracketed amongst the middle or upper middle class. Obviously, we lack the amenities and facilities found in such families. My grandmother passed away when my eldest uncle was just seven years old. Since then, it is my mother who has laboured day and night to raise my three uncles and all of us with utmost love and care, without distinction or discrimination. This is how and what my family is. You can anticipate big responsibilities coming your way.'

By deliberately painting a grim picture of our family, I had tried to test whether Kantabai understood the implication of what she had just said so eloquently. I could not believe that a graduate girl like her could actually hold traditional family values in such high esteem. She was just too agreeable—was this by design or had she been tutored? Was this a prepared script just for me? Suspicion sprang in my mind.

However, she did not seem to be rattled. True, drops of perspiration beaded her brow, and I thought tears could soon come into her eyes. But nothing of that sort happened.

'Can I offer you some water?' I inquired.

'Yes. Please, I will fetch it myself,' she said, and got up.

She handed me the glass that was meant for her, and then went inside to drink water. After putting the empty glass and tray back in the kitchen, she returned to her seat. The clock was ticking away. It was almost an hour since we had begun talking.

'I am aware of your family background. It is not totally alien to me,' she said. 'True, ours is a nuclear family today, but I have spent my entire childhood, my formative years, in a joint family. That is why I am fully aware of the implications of life in a joint family. The frequent skirmishes, the trivial arguments, the spontaneous quarrels and equally quick compromises—I am aware of all this—and have been a party to it too. And yet, I feel that a joint family is the best family system. It teaches us the value of tolerance and collective living. It creates an irreplaceable moral support system. My brother passed away in the prime of his youth. Yet, we could somehow bear the colossal loss and move on in life. Why? Because of the warmth and support of the family. After my brother's demise, I was the only child and became even dearer to my parents. But the extra love and attention did not mean undue pampering. They saw to it that I grew up valuing and imbibing the fundamental essence of a joint family. We are not financially sound today, but in those days, we were, financially and socially, the elite.'

Kantabai paused reflectively, and then resumed, 'Unable to withstand the force of the changing times, our family disintegrated. Today, there are court cases between brothers, who would once not sleep without sharing their dinner. My father is now emotionally wrecked and has become a recluse. He is unable to reconcile to the bitter realities, and lives in his glorious past, neglecting our present plight. Being kind and generous is his basic nature. He gives with a free hand even today, leaving little or nothing for the family. There are mounting court expenses to meet, and hardly any income. That I am unable to do anything to help my father nags my conscience day and night.'

'So this is my side of the story, told as candidly as you did yours. I can only say that I am certain I can handle all my responsibilities in your family competently,' she concluded.

Kantabai had spoken her mind, but her words were straight from the heart. There was no theatrical element in her narration. It mirrored her pure and unpretentious nature. Through every cross-examination, her genuineness was revealed and for once,

I was happy to lose!

'Well said! I realize that I have done most of the talking and questioning until now. Don't you want to ask me anything? If there is anything, anything at all, please feel free to ask me without hesitation.'

Kantabai sighed in relief, paused for a while, and then said, 'Not really. But there is one thing I want to say by way of clarification. I have been engaged once before. My acquaintance with that person was limited to the day of the betrothal. Thereafter, he left for America and never returned. We exchanged letters a couple of times. That is all there has ever been between him and me.'

This was the most soulful and honest admission I had ever heard in my life. However, false ideas of manliness and my lawyer mentality prevailed over my gentlemanliness, and I made a very unreasonable request, 'If possible, and if you don't mind, I would like to glance through those letters. Could you please post them to me?'

She readily agreed, 'Yes sure. But I do not have copies of the letters that I wrote to him.'

Surprise! Within a week, I got the originals—not photocopies but the original letters that that person had written to Kantabai by registered post, without any explanatory covering note. Such unconditional faith! Such trusting compliance! I read those letters many times over. Tears of repentance welled up in my eyes while reading the last letter for the third time.

What have I done? What right did I have to make such an unreasonable demand, to ask so many awkward questions, to prevail over her even before we were bound by any relationship?

My heart ached. I came from an extremely modest family. There was no toilet in my home. I slept on the floor, and studied under a feeble oil lantern. What made me think I was superior to her? Just because I was more educated and had good argumentative powers and a good command over language, I gave myself the unlimited authority to question her like a meek subject! Was this not cruelty? Was this not why women seethed to be free of dominating men for centuries? I concede, that had she asked me even half the questions that I had asked her, I would not have tolerated it. Besides, I doubted whether I would have answered them with half her honesty and transparency.

Kantabai's family was in dire straits. Her brother had passed away, and she was the only surviving child of poor, hapless and aged parents who were emotionally maimed. They hailed from Bijapur that, though historically significant, had hardly any other merit. She had already been 'branded' by the terrible social taboo of a broken engagement. No traditional man would think of getting married to her. To compound the family's misery, she was educated. Her Bachelor's degree was proving to be a curse rather than a blessing. How unfair! I pondered at the tragic irony that the same education that raised a boy's marriage credentials, could mar a girl's prospects. While it was a flowery garland for a man, it was a restrictive leash for a woman, a negative asset indeed. Such are the strange ways of our society, I rued.

Even as I was deep in thought, the memory of the graceful Kantabai invaded my conscience again and again. This young and deserving lady possessing every credential to be married to a noble, promising man, was now languishing under the prospect of remaining a spinster for life. That heartless man, who had ditched her so brazenly by writing a few lines of shameless denial, had ruined her life. Call it providence, destiny or fate, that one callous act had thrown her entire family into a sea of troubles.

No doubt, it was her father's earnest desire that Kantabai should marry me. A double-graduate boy from a good family, and good looking as well. What more could he hope for? The family must have been on tenterhooks as they awaited my reply.

Five hundred kilometres away in Wakod, I weighed the pros and cons of the situation. I liked the girl, but what if we refused the alliance? It would be like a second betrayal by a man for Kantabai. It would leave her with no other option but to remain unmarried for life. It was impossible for a Marwadi girl, no matter how qualified or cultured, to get married without a good dowry; and her father was in no position to fulfill this prerequisite. This single drawback overshadowed all other merits of the prospective bride. Knowing the situation well, Kantabai's father had made an earnest entreaty to accept this alliance. If we refused, would it not push the miserable man to suicide? The very thought shook me to the core.

I remained deeply disturbed during those days. My youthful, rebellious mind kept questioning me: Was this life after all? And if this was life, was it not unfair? One could not do what one liked to do. One could not love what is pure and beautiful, could not worship what is pious and pristine, could not utter the truth or follow what is truthful and uncorrupted. Why? Was it out of fear of family and the pressures of society, out of apprehension of losing one's prestige? Why had man become so weak and insecure? What stopped him from standing up for himself and choosing boldly and righteously? Had he so hopelessly submitted himself to social pressures that he had no other way of living except by pretension? Had he lost his own identity in this intimidating social milieu? Will he be forced to live like a hypocrite until his last breath?

No! I cannot, and I will not live such a life. Better be dead than to live with a conscience that is comatose. Of what significance is my outer existence if it cannot heed the call of the inner self? No! I will not reduce myself to such a state of subsistence at any cost.

2

IF I COULD convince mother in this entire matter, half the battle was won! I approached her early next morning at our home in Wakod, and waited for the right moment to broach the subject. It was her routine to get up at five in the morning, and by now, she had already served breakfast to father and my uncles, fetched water from the river, milked the cows and boiled the milk, and sent the children off to school with packed lunch boxes. She was churning butter with a churner that was twice her height, when I saw her humming a devotional song. I could sense her pleasant mood, and went and sat on the ladder facing her.

My mother was a born struggler. She came from Wavadde, a tiny hamlet near Jalgaon. She was illiterate, never having been to school. Her mother had passed away when she was just two, and she did not have any siblings to support her. Her father was about sixty years old then, and spent all day in a makeshift shack that doubled up as a tiny, ill-stocked grocery shop. On many days, there was no income at all. As a result, preparing even a modest meal in the evening was nearly impossible. My mother had grown up in such abject poverty! But her coming into our family after marriage proved to be very auspicious. It was as if better days followed her footsteps into our home. Soon, she started being compared to 'Lakshmi Devi', the goddess of wealth and good fortune. In particular, my uncle and aunt never tired of holding her in high esteem. She started receiving genuine respect and love from her in-laws, which was not very common in those days.

Seeing me sitting silently on the ladder, mother read what was going on in my mind, and initiated the conversation herself, 'Bhavru, which girls have you seen and what is your opinion, won't you tell your mother?'

'Maa, the Nashik girl that I saw will not suit our family.' In fact, my uncle Dalubhau had already conveyed this to mother.

'So that leaves us with the choice of the girl from Bijapur,' she said. 'But I hear that her father is in no position to offer any dowry; he cannot even bear the marriage expenses. Do they expect us to wed their daughter at our expense? This is not done.'

I came right to the point and challenged her, 'Maa, why don't you clearly say that you want dowry. And I ask you, why?'

Although illiterate, mother was shrewd and experienced in practical matters. She was about to earn the status of a mother-in-law after a lifetime of hardships and misfortunes. She had given birth to ten children, out of which eight had died an early death. I was the elder of the two surviving sons. Father was short-tempered; nobody dared open his mouth in front of him. There were three cousin brothers in the family, and four elders. Besides, there was my brother and I. It was mother who had single-handedly run the household successfully through all the ups and downs in the family. She was innately generous and kind and always ready to help the needy in the neighbourhood. She was known as the 'kind angel' in the locality. Obviously, she commanded much respect and admiration in the family and the village. On her part, she loved us, her two surviving sons, more than life itself. We would never think of going against her wishes or offending her.

Even as I argued with her on the matter of dowry, I was conscious that I may have hurt her feelings.

However, she answered me in a very composed manner.

'You give me one good reason Bhavru, why I should not ask for dowry.'

We both stuck to our guns, 'And I repeat Maa, why do you expect the dowry?'

Mother presented her logic, 'Look Bhavru, I have given dowries when I got all the girls in our family married. Now when my son is getting married, it is my turn to take a dowry. This is how it has been, and that is why my expectation is justified, I think.'

I continued the questioning, 'And is there any other reason why you want dowry?'

Mother said, 'My son is highly educated, that is one more reason.'

'Anything else?'

'What will society think if we did not get a dowry from the family of the girl?'

'Oh, okay! Any other reasons why you want a dowry?'

The churning was complete by now, and mother was collecting thick, creamy butter in another vessel. I knew that the core of her pure heart was softer than that butter, and I was determined to touch that core and tackle the matter from an emotional angle.

'Maa, you are right in your own way, but shall I put forth my view too? You will give me a kind hearing, won't you?'

Mother replied, 'How can I ignore something that the apple of my eye has to say?'

I then began my plea, 'Look mother, this concerns the Bijapur girl whose merits you are unfortunately evaluating solely from the dowry angle. I plead with you Maa, for a moment, just imagine that she was born to you in this family, and I was born in their family. You just said that this son of yours is a double graduate, good looking, sociable, and so on. The fact is that their daughter too is no less qualified and deserving. She is a graduate. She is charming, well-behaved and good-natured. Her lineage too is respectable and of good repute. Until a few years ago, they were wealthy and considered part of the elite. And her looks—Oh! You must concede that she is better looking than your son. I have wheatish complexion with an unremarkable nose, but she is fair and flawless. Beautiful doe eyes and a round attractive face. Now just think, if she were your daughter and a promising matrimonial prospect was to go away just because you could not afford a handsome dowry, how would you feel?'

My argument had Maa thinking, and she seemed to be coming around to my point of view. I decided to press further and continued, 'You are known for your compassion Maa. Why, you even give jowar free to the needy, hidden from the vigilant eyes of my uncles. You reach out to the poor expectant mothers and give them milk and buttermilk too. You sympathize with the misfortunes and sorrows of others as if they were your own. Now, if Kantabai, beautiful in body and soul—your own extension in many ways—were born to you, and if she were to face rejection just because of dowry, how dejected would you feel then Maa? Wouldn't her parents feel the same way if we reject her? Should we not be more considerate and think beyond the confines of dowry? After all, how much dowry would you expect to get from anybody? Don't you think your son is capable of earning much more than that? Do you consider the worth of a meagre dowry more than your son's aspirations and abilities? Why should we ask for a dowry at all? I am just beginning my career. I have miles to go and millions to earn, but through grit and hard work, not through this base system of dowry. Maa, you have given unconditionally all your life. You have forsaken even the money that was rightfully ours, and never taken a single paisa from anybody unfairly. I have inherited these qualities from you. I want to make you proud by earning a fortune, not by receiving it as an undeserved gift. I plead with you Maa, please support me in making my dreams come true.'

I had spoken passionately. My petition was now in mother's court. I awaited judgment with bated breath.

'Now, I see that you have really grown up and are already talking like an accomplished vakil, but don't forget that your mother is an illiterate woman of limited intellect. However, I do understand your feelings and hold them in high esteem. You have opened my eyes. If the girl's family's finances are so bad, I have no desire left for a dowry. But my son, keep in mind that your aged mother is bodily weary and withered at heart. Life's struggles have taken a heavy toll on me. I wish for someone to take over the reins of the family now. Let the situation not come to pass that some educated working madam comes home in the evening and this illiterate old woman has to serve her dinner every night.' Mother's eyes were moist as she conveyed her decision.

'Maa, trust me, I am your flesh and blood. I exist because of you. You are my creator. I will never become undeserving of your love; will never hurt your sentiments. I vow that not only I, but we—Kantabai and I—will strive to serve you with the same love and compassion with which you have served countless people. Give me your blessings so that I can live up to your expectations.' After that, I let my emotions speak, and bowed at mother's feet. She lifted me up and hugged me close to her heart.

'Now, convince the others in the family. Start preparing for the auspicious entry of "Lakshmi Devi" into our home.' We were both choked with emotion.

Till date, I do not know how I made that impassioned

plea. It was almost as if I was being inspired to speak up for a higher cause, not just out of self-interest. Whatever I am today is solely because of my parents, more so because of my mother. She raised us very virtuously and gave us impeccable sanskaar. My plea on that day was a manifestation of this cultural DNA inherited from my mother. It is indeed true that any child is an extension of his or her mother, her ideological mirror image, her elongated shadow. My simple and sincere words in fact reflected her way of thinking, and that is why they had the desired effect on her. I had spoken her language. I was truly at a loss to make out whether I had convinced her, or she had chosen to get convinced! She could well have said no, despite my earnest appeals.

Mother was pure at heart. She thought, spoke and acted the same with everyone. Double standards or double talk was totally alien to her nature. She did not discriminate, nor did she maintain one set of rules for her son, and another for the world. She respected tradition, but would not be subservient to rigid norms that had become meaningless over time.

I had three uncles. My second uncle, Dalubhau, had taken the responsibility of my university education in Bombay. He was the first university diploma holder in our family. My father had provided for his education some years ago, depriving himself of basic necessities, even food in the process. Hence, Dalubhau cared for me as he would for his own son while I stayed at their home in Ghatkopar in Bombay. He worked as an inspector in the Premier Automobile company in Kurla, earning a modest 150 rupees a month (around dollars 20 as per 1956 exchange value). While he himself wore handspun khadi, he ensured that I had good quality modern nylon clothes to wear. My aunt also looked after me with utmost love and care. It indeed was my second home in Bombay while I studied there. Out of sheer gratitude, I thought I was duty-bound to take Dalubhau into confidence on this matter. Hence, I came to Bombay to present my case to him after obtaining mother's consent.

'So Bhavru, did you meet your mother? What does she say?' Dalubhau asked.

By then, a group of eleven people under the stewardship of Dalubhau had already visited Kantabai's home in Bijapur and enjoyed their hospitality for four days. While there, they had kept the girl and her family under close observation. How she looked in various clothes, how she cooked, how she conducted herself in the house—all these matters were studied in great detail. Not only that, the team also took Kantabai's inked footprint to make sure that she was not flat-footed! Being flat-footed was not considered a good omen in those days. (The belief then was that being flat-footed was a physical disability.) They met and talked with the neighbours to get their opinion about the girl's character and behaviour outside her home. They found acquaintances from our community and questioned them about the girl. Finally, they also approached the families Kantabai used to visit often and made discreet inquiries about her from them. All this may sound very absurd today, but it was customary then to undertake such an 'in-depth due diligence' of the girl before entering into an alliance.

Dalubhau opined, 'Marriage happens once in a lifetime. Better be safe than sorry. Bringing home a bride from a totally different home has far-reaching consequences not only on the present generation, but also on future generations.'

Marriage does not just signify a bond between two persons, it also heralds the continuance of the family lineage. The quality of the future generations depends totally on the wife that brings this lineage. Hence it is of utmost importance to undertake an elaborate investigation of the bride and her family background—

this was the prevailing thought in those days. When a boy and girl got married, it also signalled the coming together of two families in a lifelong bond with far-reaching social implications. A successful marriage was a matter of pride for the families as much as it was for the couple. This set a good example in society. Given the significance that was attached to good upbringing, behaviour, conduct, understanding of household matters and the character of the girl, it was considered routine for her to pass through the tests that the boy and his near and dear ones had posed for her. This was to be borne with patience, tolerance and a willing compliance. The procedure became even more exacting, and had a touch of one-upmanship, if the boy happened to be good looking, educated and capable. Such 'merits' gave a licence to the would-be groom's kith and kin to subject the girl to any fanciful test and queries as they deemed fit, and they used this privilege freely. After all these litmus tests, a marriage, if it was finalized, came not only as a relief but an event of joy for the girl and her family. Such were those days and such were our ways.

The dialogue between Dalubhau and me was set against this background.

'Maa is concerned about two things. If the family's condition was average, then it would have been okay, but they live a hand-to-mouth existence. On top of it, the girl is a graduate. God forbid, if the girl insists on working after marriage, then Maa will have to feed her instead of the other way round. We will have to know the opinion of others in Wakod as well.' I looked at Dalubhau expectantly.

Dalubhau said, 'Bansibhau (his elder brother) has opined that if we are to stage a marriage ceremony that befits our status, we will have to do it at our cost.'

By now, I was very keen to know Dalubhau's opinion.

'Bhavru, we stayed at the girl's house for four days. We undertook several rounds of investigation and inquiries. We even consulted the headmaster of the girl's school, her friends and her neighbours. True, their financial condition is not good, but we cannot blame the girl for that in any way. And as far as her broken engagement is concerned, the girl is 100 per cent innocent. If the former is her family's misfortune, the latter is her personal misfortune. This is the unanimous opinion of all of us. If we overlook these two matters, the girl is worthy in all respects.'

The words were music to my ears. I sighed with sheer relief. Dalubhau was exposed to the liberal and cosmopolitan life of Bombay, and hence had arrived at such a fair and considered opinion. However, his demeanour did not imply that he considered this the very best or the most suitable proposal for his beloved and exceptionally qualified nephew! His unspoken expression carried a hint of reconciliation and compromise.

'So what do we do?' I inquired.

Dalubhau's response put me in a dilemma again, 'I think we should wait and watch. Meanwhile, we should take a look at a couple of other proposals. After that, we can take a final decision.'

I knew that it was Dalubhau's nature to keep postponing matters until it became absolutely unavoidable to take a decision. His attitude made me anxious, as his scepticism seemed uncalled-for.

I was a bit distressed and unnerved as I spoke, 'Uncle, we should be considerate to the girl's family even while delaying our decision. Besides, we have already decided not to prolong any decision beyond a week. So first of all, please convey our "No" to the Tonadpur and the Nashik families. As regards taking a look at a few more proposals—we really should not treat this matter casually like shopping for clothes or buying vegetables. Such a gross attitude does not behove our cultured and educated upbringing. Education should help us outgrow such an outdated mentality, rather than breed snobbery in us. Marriage is an extremely sacred alliance that determines the future of our coming generations. We should be rational when deciding on such alliances. External factors should not concern us as much as what lies at the core of a person. We should look beyond her appearance and try to probe the beauty of her qualities and character, her willingness and ability to become one with our family—just like sugar mixes with milk and makes it sweet. Please give me your independent opinion, how do you rate the girl from all these angles? She herself had broached the subject of her failed engagement during our personal talk. She was totally transparent regarding the matter. She even posted the original letters of her ex-fiancé to me upon my asking! Unbecoming though it was on my part to ask her to do so, I admire her unconditional compliance and absolute trust. What more can a person expect from another person to prove his or her innocence? Surely, we could not expect Kantabai to walk on burning coals to prove her innocence, as Sita Mata (Sita is depicted in Ramayana as an ideal wife) was made to do!

'If you are convinced of her spotless character, I would also like to tell you that she came across as a woman of high culture, ethics and values to me. I was also impressed by her instant, sound judgment. The honesty, straightforwardness, purity of intention, maturity and depth of perception that she displayed while answering each of my odd and deliberately complicated questions, were far beyond an ordinary person's capacity. I am left with no doubt that Kantabai is an extraordinary person of highest virtue. She is indeed like 24-carat gold.'

Dalubhau finally seemed convinced, but said in measured

tones, 'As such, even I think she is a good match for you. She will also adapt to our family very well. You both seem ideal and will complement each other.'

I continued, recalling my friend Pandhri's advice, 'Uncle, the dowry that one receives in marriage is expendable, the royal treatment and the hospitable overtures enacted during the ceremony may be customary, but are superficial. The VIP treatment, the lavish gifts and the rich buffet—will all be forgotten with time; none of this has any lasting value. Only the bride's qualities and character will stay with us for life. That is what makes or breaks homes. The future of the husband and the family, in totality, depends on this one person. In Kantabai's case, I am certain that she is my future and she will script my family's future in golden letters. If you agree, then let us dispel all doubts and begin the proceedings.'

We were seeing eye to eye. There was an unspoken but strong mutual agreement between us. The decision was sealed.

'Okay then, let us proceed,' Dalubhau said at last.

～

A lady named Kantabai and a gentleman named Bhavarlal were finally going to unite. The coming together was to be of body, heart and soul. The marriage was to be prophetic; it was truly made in heaven and was going to be merely formalized on earth. It was to create history.

That night, I slept soundly.

Time has changed the way many young people think about marriage and its role in life. I wonder how today's youth would deal with the circumstances that led to our engagement. Whether such an engagement would materialize at all, given the respective circumstances of the bride and the groom?

The foundation of a joint family system is based on collective welfare and sharing and caring. All tangible and intangible resources are shared equitably. Thus, the maintenance and upkeep of the family—economic or emotional—gets divided, leaving the individuals less burdened. In contrast, the small nuclear family focuses on individual advancement, and hence gives birth to larger-than-life aspirations. Couples often tend to be over-ambitious in the context of giving priority to career over family. Besides, the very concept of well-being has gained material overtones. Emotional security is linked to financial security! Couples in small families tend to be paranoid and disturbed; the more they try to gain material affluence and individual advancement, the more they seem to get isolated and fragmented as human beings.

Young girls and boys often move past the proper marriageable age in a mad rush to do better in their careers. And when good sense prevails, they are no longer marriage-worthy. Even if they do give a timely thought to marriage, they appear extremely stressed and anxious about meeting the challenge of the right choice. The shaky moral-ethical foundation and the half-baked cultural values of their nuclear families, coupled with their own immature and opportunistic approach, are at the root of this anxiety. By far, the most formidable question that looms over their decision is that of fidelity and lifelong compatibility. Failing to confront and resolve these issues regarding marriage, the youth circumvent the entire issue and decide to either remain single or to enter a live-in relationship, rather than take the risk of marriage.

For many, marriage has come to mean shackles that will tie them down to a lifelong conflict of interest and difference of opinion. It will restrain their individual advancement and pleasure. The misperceived 'lack of space' leads the husband to think that even if he gets along with his wife, will there be enough scope to nurture individual preferences under one roof? Will they get time for themselves? And what about friends? After all, they have their own place in a man's life. On the other hand, the wife thinks that the lesser the time they are together, the better it will be for both of them. If both are occupied in their own way, it will at least give them enough time for their individual pursuit of activities. And after all, she is not dependent on him financially, so her remaining with him is not need-based.

The common thread in this thinking is that one must have individual pursuits, so personal development can continue even after marriage. For this, independence is a must, even if it comes at the cost of physical and emotional detachment.

How easy it is to detach! And how challenging it is to remain attached! But the beauty of life lies in taking challenges head-on and transforming them into opportunities. What's required is an adhesive called consideration, understanding and selfless caring that will bind a relationship into a togetherness that has no agenda and is everlasting.

Marriages that are based on mutual mistrust, doubt and instability pose a big question mark on their longevity. The situation comes to such a pass that couples cannot even confide in each other with full trust and confidence. To rise above self-interest and to commit to the relationship selflessly, to reconcile and to accommodate mutual welfare in married life—these are the missing parts of the puzzle. Leave aside living happily together after marriage and developing a friendly, trusting and understanding attitude towards the spouse, and the near and dear ones; the couples fret at the very idea of shared living even between themselves! There is absolutely no room for anybody else other than I, Me and Myself in this 'sacred sanctum sanctorum' called individual space! In that space there is no room for rising above oneself and embracing another in order to create a blissful world together since the very notion is absurd and purposeless to such a mind. Marriage that is the most sacred bond on earth and a synonym of sanskaar, is viewed by such a person as a contract of convenience or an opportunist MoU (Memorandum of Understanding). One fails to understand the angle from which the youth view marriage nowadays, but one thing is certain, the view is destructive to the core since it springs from selfishness. Mindless acceptance of the western notion of individualism has landed society in deep trouble today. Our youth have strayed in the dangerous territory of individualism, forgetting our centuries-old cultural heritage of cohesive collective living. The people who have planted the deadly virus in their minds are themselves lost in the morass of materialism. Outwardly, they are affluent but empty within; they live terribly mechanical, lonely lives. In today's faceless society people crave for the human touch in their lives. Lacking in both love and commitment, marriage is a convenient prospect and appealing as long as it fulfils this hunger. But beyond this passing functionality, they don't perceive marriage to have any lasting value! Even prenuptial agreements are signed nowadays assuming that marriage is doomed to fail even before the vows are exchanged! The seriousness that higher, lifelong relationships demand is just not there. Their approach is totally 'professional' and 'practical' exactly like that towards a contact or a MoU. It is this adopted, alien approach that is eroding the institution of marriage as well as family. What is worse, man is portrayed as a cruel enemy of women and women are being positioned as pawns in his hands. The basic assumption being that they are separable! On top of it all, there is a movement to bring into effect laws regarding the personal rights and duties of each; as a result, our social fabric is quickly being ripped apart by this phenomenon of mindless aping. If allowed to spread, it is potent enough to destroy our culture, our ethos and our entire identity.

Take away our families from our lives, and what remains with us? A happy family starts with a strong marriage. Strong families build a strong nation, a strong world. And where does it all begin? A committed couple belonging to each other is indeed the nucleus of a blessed universe.

3

THE HINDU MARRIAGE system lays much stress on the betrothal or engagement ceremony. It is a system as ancient as the culture itself. In its truest sense, it 'engages' a couple in a lifelong bond. The provisions and proceedings of this centuries-old custom are identical to the Indian Contract Act 1872 that is in force even today. According to this Act, a proposal is first forwarded by one party to another in order to finalize and formalize the association. The other party then declares its acceptance of the proposal. After this, an exchange of valuables takes place that signifies the 'consideration amount' for accepting the contract. A Hindu betrothal's proceedings are exactly the same; they give the newly formed association a solemn and enduring status.

Once the families of the boy and the girl convey the acceptance of the relationship, either verbally or in writing, the girl's family visits the groom's house for the engagement ceremony with gifts for the groom-to-be and his relatives. Kantabai's father was in no position to honour this tradition on his own. He had to take a loan of 3,000 rupees from Kantabai's maternal uncle and some other people for the ceremony. This is how they could manage to offer suiting material, a wrist watch and footwear for me and some other items for the household. The ceremony was held at our home in Wakod. The entourage consisted of Kantabai's immediate family, their in-laws and Dr Jethmal Doshi, my uncle Dalubhau's classmate and close friend. The small function was attended by relatives and well-wishers from the village, and thus Kantabai and I came one step closer to lifelong togetherness.

31 May 1961, just another date in the calendar, but it became my life's most memorable day, engraved in gold on my heart! After the brief traditional ceremony, I bowed to all the elders to obtain their blessings. As per the custom, everybody gave me some cash as a token of goodwill and good luck. The offerings ranged between one and five rupees, no small amount by any means in those days. The grand total came to 57 rupees—just around one American dollar as I write this in August 2012, but it was my largest ever 'earning' then! These bank notes were mostly given by the farmers, the sons of the soil. They were soiled; some were even damp and sweaty. However, their feelings were genuine and heartfelt. I preserved this invaluable treasure of 57 rupees for many years. While the amount did not increase on its own, the affection behind it compounded a great deal with time.

There is such deep-rooted good sense in traditions and customs! Currency is nothing, it is just paper. But the paperless emotions are everything in Indian culture. God bless the good old days and the good old customs!

However, the same money that had given me a reason to hold my head high with pride for our customs, was also making it bow in utter shame. On the fringe of the festivities, a melancholy thought constantly nagged my troubled conscience.

How humiliating it must have been for Kantabai's father to ask for help in order to maintain these shallow, vain and pointless social customs. The actual cost of the suit and the watch and the shoes was his pride, self-esteem and self-respect. But how would a heartless society understand such humane considerations? Somehow because of this nagging thought, I could not bring myself to wear that suit, that watch or those shoes.

There was a time when Kantabai's father was as respected as a lord. He enjoyed celebrity status wherever he went. He could afford the exclusive luxury train coaches for the wedding of Kantabai's half-brother. A royal treatment was given to the bridegroom's party when Kantabai's older half-sister, Shantabai, got married. A 150-strong welcome committee was deployed at the railway station just to receive the groom's entourage! For such a man, to seek help for Kantabai's engagement expenses! How do men of conscience tolerate such customs? How can such customs that can break a man's spine into tiny splinters, continue? The sheer humiliation of it can take his self-respect away forever. What is left of him thereafter?

The sight of Kantabai, weeping silently and trying desperately to prevent the tears from wetting her eyelashes, will never leave my memory. It was an occasion for rejoicing and yet there was sorrow. In those days, the bride's father was a hapless victim of a society that was subjugated by rigid customs. He would go to any lengths to measure up to society's expectations while getting his daughter married. My family was no exception to this social charade. How could it ever succumb to the custom of dowry? Perhaps, this bitterness would have gradually left my heart had things stopped there.

It is said that when troubles come, they come in pairs. Just three or four days after our betrothal, I received an anonymous letter claiming that Kantabai had had a discreet affair with a Maharashtrian neighbour. The letter pierced my heart like a thunderbolt. It rattled me to the core. I could compromise on anything, but not on character. I was extremely disturbed. Obviously, I lost many nights of sleep over the issue.

For my family, my choice of Kantabai was considered almost a compromise. First, there was the matter of her family's financial condition. Then came the matter of her failed engagement, tarnishing her 'marriage-worthiness'. And lastly, they lived in far-off Bijapur, which was socially alien to us. However, my family had discarded all these notions and had firmly supported my decision. But, what if I was proved wrong in my choice? The burden of accountability lay heavily on me. On the other hand, Kantabai's family was also apprehensive that after having being brought up in a town like Bijapur, would she be able to settle down in a tiny, nondescript village. Also, the burden of a large extended family to be borne single-handedly. Would it not be an unfair marriage for her? Did she not deserve better?

Nevertheless, Kantabai was as steadfast in her decision as I was. She had detached herself from the whole unsavoury episode of the anonymous letter and had maintained a dignified silence.

Dr Jethmal Doshi was a frequent visitor to my uncle Dalubhau's home. In fact, he had played a key-mediating role in our engagement. Somehow, I just could not get that anonymous letter out of my head, and decided to refer the matter to Dr Doshi and ask him if he could call Kantabai to Nashik for a heart-to-heart talk. He immediately sent for Kantabai who was in Malegaon paying a visit to her maternal uncle there, and called me to Nashik too.

As soon as I reached Nashik, I asked Kantabai who her neighbours were in Bijapur and who among them might have written that anonymous letter.

Meanwhile, Pushpabai, Dr Doshi's wife, who was Kantabai's niece, came to my help. She said, 'Both you and I are from Jalgaon, so I am morally obliged to give you my honest opinion regarding Kantabai's character. With utmost sincerity and with my hand on my heart, I can vouch that Kantabai possesses a spotless character. This anonymous letter is nothing more than a cheap, malicious act to cause mischief. I plead with you, please trust me.'

Pushpabai's honest and truthful words acted like balm to my aching heart.

In those days, the practice of writing anonymous letters with a malicious intention was not limited to the dirty games played by royalty. This practice was rampant among the morally corrupt social elements that derived sadistic pleasure from its disastrous consequences. These worms of society feasted on character assassination. Obviously, the gullible, lacking in conviction, would easily fall prey to such conspiracies and forsake their own bright future. I, too, could have done the same and could have said to myself, 'Better safe than sorry'. However, Kantabai answered each of my queries with utmost honesty and transparency. I was ultimately convinced of her unblemished character. I reassured her that my decision was firm and final, come what may.

I felt calm, happy and contented. After all the problems, I was to wed the girl of my choice. I returned to Bombay with this firm conviction.

4

THE GROOM'S ENTOURAGE left Wakod and reached Nashik via Pachora. The chief host on this occasion was obviously Dr Jethmal Doshi, without whose earnest initiatives this relationship would never have materialized. It was because of him that this Prince Charming was standing at the doorstep of his Cinderella. The ceremonies and rituals seemed endless and I was impatient to sweep my bride off her feet and escape to a world of our own.

Dr Doshi was then the chief medical officer of Nashik Central Jail. Initially, Kantabai's family wanted to hold the marriage at Bijapur as per custom. But then, they would have had to incur all the expenses of the groom's entourage. For a marriage party of fifty, the two-way fare alone would have been punishing for Kantabai's father. I thought of a way out and suggested we hold the marriage in Nashik, which was accepted amiably by both parties. Dr Doshi's kind consideration and services once again saved the situation, as we could use his place and facilities for the marriage ceremony.

Those gracing the ceremony from the bride's side included the Kothari family from Poona, the Mutha family from Bombay, Dr Doshi and his family and friends, and distinguished community members from Nashik. The bride's maternal uncle and his family were also present.

In many contemporary societies, the marriage ceremony and the accompanying rituals have become a boring compulsion tolerated just to get the 'licence' of marriage. Marriage itself, however, has become an expendable contract of convenience with a limited purpose and function. Even its time frame is open-ended. The contract can be dissolved at the slightest hint of inconvenience to either partner. Physical compatibility has gained overriding consideration in such short-lived relationships. Such bonds get shattered once the physical attraction wanes. Thus, the fabric of marriage becomes faded, its lustre and sheen having worn out. With the passage of time, one of the most sacred of human ties has been reduced to carnal desires. Obviously then, the holy rituals and symbolic customs carried out to solemnize such weddings have lost all their relevance and significance.

In contrast, the sanctity of the Hindu marriage still retains its piousness and solemnity. Anybody attending a Hindu marriage will not miss the air of gravity surrounding the bride and groom as they dedicate themselves to each other for life. It is an everlasting association that transforms 'the self' into 'the selfless'; it is the harbinger of grihasthashram or the phase of committed domesticity in life, which is typified by unconditional caring and sharing. The hymns and the chants recited during the ceremony reiterate the solemnity of the event as well as the solidarity of the couple and call for celestial consent for the newly formed marriage. For example, during the ritual of Akshat Ropan, both the bride and groom express their desires to each other while sprinkling purified rice seeds anointed with auspicious kumkum (red pigment), amidst sacred chanting. These wishes do not reflect just the material and worldly aspirations, they also seek commitment, fidelity and sacrifices for the sake of shared aims. These strong virtues form the genesis of a Hindu marriage. That is why perhaps they withstand all odds in life.

Vivah Sanskaar, or virtuous matrimony, is at the centre of the Hindu thought of ideal domestic life, which consists of a total of thirty-six qualities. The nature and future of the new life that would result from the marriage is predicted on the basis of the 'compatibility score' of the couple. Astrologers are customarily consulted before finalizing a matrimonial alliance. They study the horoscopes of both the bride and the groom and rank their compatibility on a scale of one to thirty-six. A score of eighteen is the minimum score required, while the higher scores indicate a progressively better matrimonial life. Ironically, the score of a perfect thirty-six is not considered good. It is believed to be too idealistic or too good to be true. Two equals can create animosity as easily as they can create amity. Nowadays such talk of horoscope-based matchmaking is considered as humbug by the modern youth, but I beg to differ. Astrology is an ancient science, and there is much sense in it. In our case, the astrologers had calculated a compatibility score of thirty after studying our horoscopes. Our blissful companionship of four decades stands testimony to my belief in this science. What more can I ask for from a belief system that recommended Kantabai as my soulmate?

Our marriage was fixed for 4 December 1961. Dr Doshi had taken prior permission from the jailer of the Nashik jail to hold our marriage in its premises. The venue seemed providential to me. I was to serve a 'life term' in Kantabai's captivity!

Winters in Nashik are very cold. However, I was unmindful of the late evening chill. The anticipation of seeing the bride's face warmed my heart. My eagerness grew as the auspicious moment of solemnization drew closer. I was wearing the traditional three-piece royal wedding outfit consisting of a sherwani, a richly embellished knee-length coat, skin-tight pants hooked at the bottom and an opulent embroidered scarf on my shoulders. A matching turban with a peacock feather adorned my head. I was nervous and excited in equal measure as I mounted a horse for the first time in my life. On cue, the waiting street band started playing loud, jovial music and everybody broke into dance. Firecrackers added to the noisy gaiety. The air was thick with the smell of rose water that was being sprinkled on the procession. The syce loosened the rein and the horse began its steady trot. Bhavarlal was finally on his way to meet Kantabai, this time, forever.

As the procession reached the jail, an inevitable thought came to my mind. This was the end of being single. I was about to give up my independence and embrace a shared life with a partner of my choice. Taking an objective view, it was a good deal. I was getting married at an opportune time. The same way as a hedge of wild plants stops the soil of a field from being washed away and wasted in the monsoon, a timely marriage channelizes one's emotional and physical energies towards the creation of an ideal family and a healthy society. It stops the mind from straying and engages it in working productively to achieve the desired goals. A man can never achieve his material, idealistic and spiritual goals singly, as he can with a supportive life partner. The wife is truly a man's better half. Besides, in my case, I instinctively knew that our marriage was also going to play a larger role and become instrumental in serving society in addition to the family and the community. This thought became more acute as the auspicious moment drew closer. Why so? Perhaps, it was a timely reminder from the heavens about my imminent social responsibilities that were going to be fulfilled through this marriage. I also had an intuitive feeling that if we could manage our domestic affairs well and engage with society meaningfully, we would successfully carry out an exalted purpose. Realization dawned on me then, that providence had embedded societal cause in our marriage. Henceforth, we were to live not only for our own good, but for the good of others too.

The procession was steadily progressing towards the marriage venue. My thoughts also progressed—what if the institution of marriage did not exist? Can a man blend well with society singly, without a woman? And even if he could, would he be received warmly by society? Was it not momentous that such thoughts occurred to me just as I was about to get married? They reconfirmed my unshakable faith in marriage as a primary pillar of strength for any society.

Marriages can be of many types. There are those that are performed purely for material considerations. Then there are those that are pretentious and serve only the pseudo-social cause. Worse are the marriages that are performed to bury a decadent past or to hide one's dark secrets. All such marriages fail miserably, bringing down the couple and the families. Besides, they tarnish the image of the institution of marriage and reduce its credibility. In contrast, principled and virtuous couples who remain committed to themselves, their families and their society, ultimately help create a better world.

I vaguely recollect a phrase coined by a Western playwright, 'Marriage is a public confession of a strictly private intention'. Indeed, this thought befits the materialist and sensual mindset very well. I feel very distressed when I see such alien thoughts corrupting the minds of our youth. We are a cultured society with very deep moral roots. How could we be shaken so easily by external forces? For those who equate a marriage's worth and purposefulness with mere physical compatibility, my thoughts will appear to be orthodox, even archaic. I am well aware of this section of thinkers. To them, I have only this much to say: the societies that have belittled the institution of marriage in a senseless rush for material gain have rapidly become decadent. These are the cultures that are deeply disturbed from within. Nothing remains of their moral core reducing their people to mere emotional weaklings. They are constantly gripped by fear and insecurity that a personal catastrophe may strike their lives and destroy them any time. They are not at all sure about their tomorrows. That is why they promote self-destructive concepts of 'living in the present' and 'living on the edge', which push them into the abyss of total ruination. I am grieved to see this phenomenon spreading like wildfire amongst our youth. Can we not offer them a secure environment where they can feel safe? Can we not offer them affectionate, happy families?

Space between four walls is merely trapped emptiness. It is the homemaker who adds a soul to it and transforms it into a happy home. She nurtures a home like she nurtures her little ones; she considers it her own extension, and builds it with utmost care, concern and commitment. A virtuous woman's soul is that womb from which happy families are born. Even at the risk of sounding repetitious, I will emphasize that the future of one's entire lineage depends on the cultural and biological DNA of the homemaker. That is why a wedding is given ritualistic importance in our culture. It is a purification process; it is like the pious Ganges which absorbs all the flaws and follies, drawbacks and negativities, weaknesses and shortcomings of both the bride and the groom, and prepares them for a model matrimonial life. From a different angle, marriage symbolizes a gateway in time, crossing which, the couple leaves behind its past forever and enters into a new life, to create a new life. A promising, common future cannot be created unless the couple comes together in body, heart and soul. Two individuals cannot create life until they become one.

Husbands and wives who fail to unite thus experience perpetual incompleteness in their lives. The reason is simple. They lack in transparency. They don't trust fully and unconditionally, but expect to be trusted. My talk about transparency and trustworthiness may sound too idealistic in today's times, but a happy matrimony cannot be created without trust, faithfulness and commitment. They are the building blocks of morally upright marriages. Yesterday, today, tomorrow; and for generations to come. If ever the soul is to reside in marriages, families and homes, it will find its way through these virtues. This is one cardinal rule that changing times or changing values will never be able to change.

Transparency is that concrete mixture which reinforces the strength of a marriage's foundation. Only when this foundation is strong, will the edifice of domesticity stand tall, straight and proud, only then will it be unblemished and unaffected by external influences.

The procession ended after meandering through Nashik's roads for about forty-five minutes. With it, my thoughts also ended.

After a warm welcome at the gate, we were seated in the canopied marriage venue. The pre-marriage rituals began amidst much gaiety. Next came the turn for the Bad Bhoj ritual, a tradition where the groom is served a feast with which he pretends to get upset and demands expensive gifts as his price for reconciliation. I was averse to this custom and flatly refused to enact the required theatrics. How can money ever equate with sanskaar?

In those days, marriages did not include extravagances like videography, flowers and fragrances, lengthy speeches and stage dancing. I have only one photo of my marriage, that too with Kantabai's face hidden behind the ceremonial veil!

The main ritual of the couple taking the seven sacred nuptial vows, symbolically witnessed by the Fire God, was accomplished. A dinner was hosted for the groom's entourage, after which we retired for the day in the special quarters arranged for us. Kantabai obviously accompanied me. Nonetheless, as soon as we reached our room, she retreated to join her family! I say, what kind of teasing was this! What a betrayal! For once, I was not in agreement with tradition! Next morning, however, I was allowed 'possession' of her after some more teasing from the bride's family. We left for Wakod by the noon train. The married couple was to travel in an exclusive first-class coupe, while the others went in a third-class compartment.

The bride's farewell is an emotionally charged moment in an Indian wedding. Streaming tears run down puffy red eyes as the bride says goodbye to her near and dear ones. The atmosphere gets extremely solemn. The most moving moments are those when the bride bows to her parents, seeks their blessings and asks for their permission to leave. No daughter on earth would miss saying a silent prayer for the welfare of her parents as she steps out of their home for the last time and takes the first few tentative steps towards her husband and her future. As she says goodbye to everyone, it is as if she begins her second avatar in the same life. In the case of Kantabai, the gravity of the situation was magnified many times. She had been her parents' only support after her two half-sisters got married, whose husbands were not very sympathetic to the family's plight. Under these circumstances, who would look after them, care for them, once Kantabai left as well? There was a big question mark about their future, and it weighed heavily on me. I felt crestfallen, almost guilty of a wrongdoing. I too cried silently.

There is an evergreen Hindi film song: 'Doli Chadh Ke Dulhan Sasural Chali' (the bride mounts the palanquin and begins her journey to her matrimonial home). The lyrics of this song are intense and laden with emotion. I could gauge their full impact only when I witnessed first-hand the pain of a daughter's separation from her parents—that too, under such conditions.

A woman is gifted with infinite amounts of courage, resilience and endurance. While bestowing upon her the paramount responsibility of settling down in a totally new household, destiny also gives her strength and resilience to do so. Some view this responsibility as a curse; I see it as a unique privilege that makes women superior to men in many ways. Would men ever pass the acid tests that women do?

Life after marriage is a totally new experience for a woman. Each household has its peculiar lifestyle, its own routine, its own flow. The day begins and ends in a different manner in every household. Add to this the family norms, traditions, preferences and viewpoints of different family members. To adjust to this enormous change overnight—only an Indian bride can perform this near-impossible feat. The Change Management gurus have a lesson to learn from this 'case study' in this era of globalization! Many women get shattered in the process; they are unable to come to grips with the situation, they become helpless before the enormity of the challenge. Many of them give up. Yet most, like Kantabai, survive the rigours and ultimately become one with the family, just like perfume mixes with the air to make the whole atmosphere fragrant. They do so by choice, not by compulsion. They win on the strength of their amiable personality and tact, not by forceful insistence or by rigid conflict. They care genuinely and they sacrifice selflessly. They face every challenge with a smile, and they adapt to every situation with mature understanding. This is how they make an alien home their own.

I felt extremely lucky to have Kantabai as my life partner. Nonetheless, a certain amount of uncertainty entered my thoughts as we proceeded to the railway station—was life to become a song or a shrill cry hereafter? But I reined in my thoughts immediately.

By the time we settled down in our coupe, both of us had composed ourselves. Romance was in the air. The veil was now lifted, and I was viewing Kantabai as my wife for the first time. Man and woman had now become husband and wife. Two souls, separate entities until that moment, were ready to merge into everlasting oneness. We engaged in an affectionate embrace. A thought passed my mind—I had now truly become 'four-armed'. My strength had doubled. So had my ability to dream and to make my dreams come true.

Our train journey terminated at Pachora in the dead of night. From here on, we were to travel to Wakod by road. The cold was severe and biting. The station master offered the comfort of the waiting room for the bride and my elderly parents. However, nobody moved from their places. Kantabai, too, remained glued to her seat. This was her first test of endurance in an endless chain that was to follow! She had chosen to wed into a family where there was culture of continuous hard work, discipline and dogged determination to achieve aims.

Life in Wakod was worlds apart from Bijapur. Kantabai was accustomed to asphalt roads, electricity, tap water and toilets and bathrooms in the house. These amenities were unheard-of in her new home. In Bijapur, she lived in a bungalow, no matter how old, while almost all homes in Wakod including ours were mud-dwellings. They would also invariably be adjoining smelly cattle sheds. The village roads were nothing more than wobbly dirt tracks with sewerage flowing in open gutters on both sides or sometimes even in the centre of the road.

The chores, too, would need the day to be of twenty-eight hours to get completed! Right from labouring at a manual flour mill, to washing the clothes of a dozen family members at the riverbank, to cleaning the utensils thrice a day, to cooking as much as for a community…the list was endless. And all this was to be managed almost single-handedly! Kantabai was indeed a gutsy woman to have married me! There is more. The postman visited our village once every four days, and the concept of reading newspapers was non-existent. Wakod was in the hinterland of India, a far cry from Bijapur. Sleepy and dusty, cut off from the mainstream, a world of its own. Its menfolk tilled the fields in the mornings, rather than reading newspaper headlines; most of them could not read anyway! The women made breakfast and milked the cows and churned the butter rather than taking leisurely morning baths.

Only time would tell how Kantabai dealt with this unfamiliar life, and how she overcame every challenge.

5

I WAS TO APPEAR for my second year LLB exams at the Nashik centre. Dr Doshi was on a family vacation in Delhi then, so I had to hire a room in Rajkamal Hotel. I needed to prepare intensely for the exam for at least six weeks, hence Kantabai and I left for Nashik early. It turned out to be an opportunity in disguise for our second honeymoon! It was also to be our first and last stay together for six long weeks, if one discounts the Wakod and Jalgaon days.

I immersed myself in books. Outings and merrymaking took a backseat. I realized that this was the best and perhaps the only chance to understand each other better, to know each other's shortcomings and temperament. To build bridges over differences, reconcile to new realities, to complement and supplement each other's role in this new life, to overcome individual weaknesses and to be each other's strength. During those intimate heart-to-heart dialogues, we touched upon the mistakes of the past and worked out ways on how not to repeat them. Rather than going to parks and sharing ice creams, we created flowery dreams for our future life—we shared objectives for king-size plans and objectives in that tiny 10'x12' room. At least in one respect, I was the greater beneficiary—they did not cost me anything!

In this manner, we created a very private paradise of bliss and became like children without any pretension and duality. We were children, unknown to pretension and duality. And because of that childlike innocence and transparency, we could understand each other with absolute clarity. Physically, we were both short. But together, we became taller than the lengthy shadows of doubt and mistrust that so often eclipse so many marriages.

Those six weeks of cozy togetherness were memorable, precious and priceless. There was absolutely no pressure on either of us to act, behave or talk in any prescribed way. We were independent adults with our own opinions as far as our exchange of ideas was concerned, and a powerful collective force of emotion and intellect as far as our resolve to achieve our goals was concerned.

Nothing was planned. Nothing was artificial. There was no effort to hide anything; the need simply did not arise. We just went wherever the current of spontaneous talk took us. The outcome invariably was a firm resolve to live for each other, for others, until our last breath. The resolve that came out of such intimate moments was pure, transparent and firm.

Along with my LLB exam, we were also getting ready for the challenging life that the heavens had scripted for us.

Dr Doshi diagnosed me with jaundice soon after my exams were over. He had returned to Nashik by then, and insisted that we stay back for treatment at his home. Our departure for Jalgaon was accordingly delayed by two weeks.

Our new home in Jalgaon was rented at 16 rupees per month (around one-third US dollar by 2012 valuation!). It was a modest two-room apartment located in Tijori Gali. Hand in hand, Kantabai and I stepped into that 'dream home'. I can never forget those early days of pleasure and pain, shared equally.

Within just four to five months, a disheartening event occurred. It taught me an invaluable lesson on domestic life in a joint family, and I share it here with all my young friends so that they can learn how to deal with situations such as these that will invariably occur in their married lives as well.

I had gone out after dinner for some work. When I returned at about 10.30 p.m., I was taken aback to find Kantabai distressed and crying. This was only the second time that I had seen tears in her eyes—the first being her farewell to her family after marriage. I was distraught to see her in such a state. Kantabai's weeping was unstoppable, so I said, 'Stop crying first. Have some water and gather yourself together, so that we can talk.'

When she returned, I asked what had happened.

She then started venting her anguish. It was as if the floodgates of her dammed-up emotions were released. My mother and other family members had reprimanded her earlier in the day, without any cause, and for no fault of hers. Their tone was unjustifiably and unpardonably harsh, demeaning and hurtful. As her outburst continued, I remained silent and listened intently. I could see that there was more hurt and anguish than anger in her words. She even said that at this rate, it would be difficult for her to live in such an emotionally claustrophobic environment. I understood her feelings and agreed with her fully.

I told her consolingly, 'Such incidents are bound to happen in a joint family. I want to know from you what should be done to arrive at a permanent solution.'

'What do I know,' she replied curtly. She still sounded deeply hurt.

'Then take heed to what I have to say to you,' I said.

'Look, I have been a member of this family much before you became a part of it, so I know it better than you. I can vouch that none of my family members are wicked or ill meaning. As for my parents, please understand that I exist because of them, they created me. Without them, you would not be here, because I would not have existed. I will remain indebted to my parents forever for giving me this life and for raising me to the best of their ability. I am what I am because of their countless sacrifices. They have often gone to sleep on an empty stomach so that I could pay my tuition fees. Gratitude is a virtue very close to my heart. I can never be ungrateful to anybody, least of all to my parents. When you have heartfelt gratitude for somebody, politeness and courteousness automatically follow. It is of paramount importance that we treat our elders with utmost politeness and respect, irrespective of their behaviour. Respect and compassion for elders are at the root of our culture. You yourself have said that it gives you tremendous inner joy to serve the elders, and I agree with you fully. As far as reconciling with elders is concerned, it is more advisable to change ourselves rather than expect them to change at an advanced age. We must understand their mindset and age-related physiological and psychological state. We will be able to overlook and overcome our hurt and pain once we start understanding our elders from this perspective.'

I noticed that my reasoning was having a positive impact on Kantabai. Her head was bowed in resignation and distress when I had begun, but now she sat up and was listening intently.

I continued, 'It is easy to destruct, but extremely challenging to construct. And as you know, I have always chosen the challenging path. I am confident that you will succeed in keeping this family united and undivided. But for this, you will have to make supreme sacrifices. You will have to give a lot before you start to get anything back in return. This does not mean that you will have to forgo your identity, your worth and your esteem totally. Just contain your uprightness and forthrightness initially, even if you know you are not at fault. Be tactful while dealing with my family, act prudently and pragmatically. And yes, always accept your mistakes readily and rectify them graciously. If you are able to do this much, then misunderstandings will be nipped in the bud. Refrain from answering back and adopting a tit for tat attitude. Restrain your temper. If you are patient and persistent, and maintain a silent but stoic dignity, then these same people will soon start adoring you. They will start treating you as Lakshmi, as you so rightfully deserve to be treated. They will look up to you for even their smallest needs. Doubtless, you will become indispensable to the family in the next four to five years. But to go to the extent of separating from the family because of such an incident, to bake our own bread and to eat lonely meals, I think is totally uncalled-for. In any case, I will never be able to stoop to such depths of ingratitude.'

I had spoken passionately, with conviction. But soon I realized that my words might have rattled her confidence, whereas the need of the hour was to build her faith and confidence in my family and me. I tried to mend matters, 'To put it differently, I am only trying to be "debt-free" from all family obligations by serving them and doing my duties. But you are better than me in this respect. So you tell me, how we can do our bit for the family in a better manner?' She was quite composed by now. Perhaps she was convinced that her husband would never be unconcerned about her feelings and what she had to say. So she spoke out, 'I am only saying that if I am at fault, they can scold me, correct me! But to be subjected to such unprovoked behaviour without any reason…how would you feel if you were in my place? Won't you feel like a dumb animal? Will such a life not be worthless?'

I could see her point of view, and the picture was clear. At the same time, I was firm that such trivial incidents should not be allowed to shatter the peace of the family. Agreed, the elders often don't treat their daughters-in-law in the right manner, but they don't do so intentionally. They belong to the previous generation. Their conduct is governed by archaic, preconceived ways; their psyche is conditioned by convention, and it is not easy to break free from these conventions at sixty, seventy or eighty plus. So who adjusts and adapts? The younger generation does. The thick trunk of an aged tree can never bend, only a young plant can. Elders are great assets to the family. The worth of their experience, wisdom and pragmatism is beyond measure. Their untold sacrifices have made it possible for us to do better in life. Young couples have to acknowledge their presence in the family, treat them with respect and lovingly care for them. They deserve to feel needed. Today's sons and daughters-in-law will be tomorrow's parents-in-law. What then?

I was facing the uphill task of convincing my wife about all this, but for the time being, she seemed to be in a state of denial. I put a comforting arm around her shoulder, and answered her question gently, 'No, I don't think so. Life can never become worthless just because two utensils collide and there is some noise in the house. Rather than getting offended with the elders, we should understand the broader context of their behaviour. Their age and level of literacy, the sociocultural and economic background in which they were brought up—if we view their behaviour in this context, we will be able to understand them better. How would we conduct ourselves if we were in their place? With this appreciation comes respect and reverence for them, and then it becomes easy to overlook their behaviour and see the brighter side of the picture. We should not judge them on the basis of their conduct alone. We are literate and educated. We can evaluate a situation from multiple perspectives. It is expected of us to be broad-minded and large-hearted. If we cannot be sympathetic towards our own elders, how can we expect others to be so? These are early days for you in the family. Be patient. As I make progress, as the gloom of misfortune disappears from over the family's roof, and as you settle down, the sense of belonging will come automatically. You will be able to win everybody's hearts with your patience, perseverance and large-heartedness.'

Kantabai's resentment and anguish now took the form of confrontation, 'Why are you so confident that I will be able to bear it all so easily?' Right from our first meeting, I knew that she was very articulate, so I resorted to reason, 'On the basis of our pre-marriage meetings, and more so, on the basis of our lengthy discussions during our Nashik sojourn, I am not just hopeful, but certain that you will be able to do so! You just need to accept my counsel as your own conviction. After mother, the family's reins will be in your hands. Start cultivating the feeling of ownership right from now and you will see an astonishing transformation taking place in your outlook and attitude. Once you start belonging here, the family will automatically start belonging to you. None amongst my family or relatives are cunning or conniving and none will ever hurt you knowingly, take that from me as a promise.'

Kantabai seemed to understand. I could feel that my talk had made sense to her. But I did not want to rush her. Very soothingly, I told her, 'In varying degrees, my people are straightforward, uncomplicated and pure at heart. Think about what I have said calmly. At the end of it, if you still feel that it is beyond you to handle the family and its affairs, we will revisit the subject and find a way forward. Alternatively, let us switch our roles. I will take on the domestic responsibilities. But in that case, I will have to give up my ambition of establishing a vast, global business. It will be like aborting our biggest dream. Will your heart ever accept that? Instead, let us work on dividing our responsibilities in such a manner that we get to do what we are best at, what we are meant for, what we have come together to do. Will that not be a better way to unite the family with the business—and the business with the family? Who do you think is better suited to undertake this? This is a delicate issue in our lives and I have to make it happen.'

Just as I finished that sentence, I suddenly realized that I was talking about 'dividing' rather than 'sharing'. For a moment, I had forgotten that there was no 'you' and 'me' between us. There was only 'us'. Having realized the mistake, correction took place automatically, 'If we are able to share our responsibilities with mature understanding, we will manage both. We will be able to build a vast, flourishing enterprise that will provide a living to thousands of families, and we will also succeed in keeping our joint family intact with our love, dedication and care. Such things happen only by divine providence. Can the chariot of domesticity ever progress on one wheel? You are nurturing our first child in your womb. Any distress on your mind will adversely affect our progeny.'

It appeared that the intensity of her grief had receded significantly. She must have realized that her husband had candidly highlighted some of his grand plans for their future.

'I realize my mistake. It will not be repeated. I will accept total responsibility of the family from now on.'

My heart received her simple words just like the scorched earth receives the first showers. The conversation, which had started with feelings of distress and alienation, ended with the union of eager lips. All tension and stress melted away in those golden moments of reconciliation.

6

IT WAS 1962, the last week of May. The Jalgaon heat was at its peak. As usual, I reached home late, and by the time dinner was over it was around 11.30 p.m. Kantabai had willingly taken it upon herself to serve me fresh, hot rotis for dinner, no matter what the time was. It became an unfailing daily routine; her symbolic way of expressing dedication and love for me. As such, this was a typical Brahmin custom (Brahmins are considered the descendants of Lord Brahma; the highest priestly Hindu caste) to serve the husband so dedicatedly, hence I used to bask in this 'Brahminic' pampering! I still recollect the Brahmin couple living opposite us indulging in such mealtime togetherness. Though, with a difference; theirs was at a decent hour of around 10.30 to 11:30 in the morning, while ours was at an unearthly hour, late night, when half the world around us was fast asleep!

At times, a weary Kantabai would doze off while waiting for me. But my footsteps would invariably jolt her awake, and she would immediately light the chullah (small coal-fired oven) to prepare rotis. Kantabai's standing complaint was that I used to fall into deep, restful sleep within minutes of having such a satisfying dinner, while she lay awake, disturbed by my snoring. I would then file a counter-complaint saying that her steady snoring interrupted my sleep too! Though, it would be pre-dawn by then and I would have completed my first spell of blissful sleep. However, we would forget our complaints by mutual consent at daybreak, and a new day of idyllic domesticity would dawn in our lives.

One night, however, it was exceptionally hot. I woke up at about 12.30 a.m. or so, as I was feeling the heat, and I saw that Kantabai had made a fan out of a piece of cardboard. She pretended to be fanning herself, but it was actually directed at me!

I asked, 'What's the matter, why aren't you sleeping?'

'No, you woke up early today, so I'm missing the lullaby of your habitual snores! As it is, I am fatter than you, so the heat is making me perspire more. I thought fanning would bring some relief.'

'But you are fanning me,' I said.

'No big deal. We are sharing the cool breeze, just as we share everything else! Besides, I'm used to fanning like this in summer.'

Our two-roomed apartment was occupied by our family of eight or nine. One room was exclusively allotted to us—the newly married couple. The rest had to accommodate themselves on the verandah or terrace, though mostly on the terrace. I had a table of 1'x5' in that small room of 10'x10', which was my 'office', with an antiquated black phone sitting on it! A 'bookshelf' was cut into the wall, which was always overstuffed with reading material.

The modest home reflected our strained financial condition. We could hardly make ends meet, even with stocks of wheat, jowar and ghee coming from Wakod. The gap between demand and supply was large and growing, what with a steady flow of guests. Nathibai, a relative, joined the family for a long stay recuperating after a surgery. Jadavbai also came in from Nasirabad. Kantabai had to 'stretch' resources by adding an equal amount of water to the milk and do other such jugglery with the groceries.

Nonetheless, there was never a frown on her face or

discontent in her heart. She had embraced the family as her own. She always upheld its pride and esteem.

We had taken a joint decision to have our children within the first five to seven years of our marriage. We wanted to devote the rest of our lives to raising them in the best possible manner, and in realizing our other dreams. Pregnant with our first child, Kantabai brought good luck to me and to the family. In February 1963, I was allotted an agency for kerosene from the Esso company, which I named 'Jain and Brothers'. Soon thereafter, I was given agencies for two petrol pumps that I named 'Ajintha Traders, Pahur'. Was providence finally smiling on us through Kantabai? The good fortune was very opportune, it proved right the adage: 'The blind seeks just one eye with vision, but divinity favours him with both eyes'.

Kantabai became our lucky charm. Good fortune kept smiling on us like the full moon showers its soothing moonlight on earth. My parents would sing Kantabai's praises to whoever would listen to them. Irrespective of the fact that such praise had any rational basis, it was customary for the elders in those days to blow their daughter-in-law's trumpet throughout the town saying how propitious her coming into their household had been. All this positivity did have a favourable effect on the psyche of an expectant Kantabai. It was believed in those days that the harder an expectant mother works, the better her chances will be of a normal delivery. Kantabai had no shortage of hard work, and to add to this, she was being hailed as an angel. The good effects of all this did help her carry her baby to a full, healthy term.

The memories of those early days in Tijori Gali are unforgettable. We did not have a cooking gas connection then; all cooking was done on wood fire or on a chullah. It was a nightmare for Kantabai to cook under such conditions. She would have vomiting fits due to the smoke and the strain. Given her condition, asking hopefully, 'What are you cooking today?' and expecting several types of dishes was out of question. My brother Kantilal and I doubled up as part-time cooks whenever circumstances demanded. It was the least we could do for the selfless lady who had ignored all personal hardships and served the family with utmost love and dedication. Such small gestures of help and support went a long way in strengthening Kantabai's and the family's closeness during those difficult days.

My wife delivered our first child at Dr Chandrikabai Desai's maternity home on 10 February 1963. I had been in Bombay for around ten days then, and could only return to Jalgaon three or four days after the baby's birth. Although my absence at such a time should have upset Kantabai a lot, there was not a trace of dissatisfaction on her face or a complaint on her lips. She understood my heavy responsibilities during those formative days of our business, and restrained her inner feelings rather well. She had, anyhow, reconciled herself to my giving preference to business commitments over family and social life.

I went straight to the maternity home after I returned to Jalgaon. I shall never forget my first sight of her on that day. Her face was beaming, glowing with the pride of becoming a mother for the first time, radiating joy and contentment as one does only after accomplishing a mission. The relatives slipped away one after the other as I entered the room. I realized that this was the first time we were meeting as parents! I was too overwhelmed. It was difficult to find words to express my emotions. For quite some time, all I could do was to keep shifting joyful glances from the newborn to the mother, and then back to our infant child. And all she could do was to smile shyly from the corner of her eyes. I drew the curtains. Our lips were eagerly awaiting each other.

I stroked her cheeks and embraced her. It was then that I had to tell her, 'I need to go now but will be back soon.'

The Jalgaon heat was fierce, even in early February. Luckily the nursing home had installed a large Crompton fan in the room. But what after the mother and child came home? Our house did not have a fan, and buying one was wishful thinking, in my dreams but out of my means. I seethed with frustration, but somehow consoled my guilt-ridden heart by thinking that the summer would soon be over and then the climate would cool down during the monsoon. So where was the need for a fan? However, my mother did not accept the situation so readily.

'Bhavru, should we not have a fan at home? The mother and child will roast in this heat. Just see if something can be managed.' But I pretended not to hear her.

This was from my mother whose life had been an endless story of struggle. She had spent her entire life under a tin roof. Charcoal fumes had choked her youthful aspirations, and her fate was smeared by the soot of wood fire! Yet, she was now fretting at the thought of her daughter-in-law and first grandson suffering due to the heat.

Where else can such golden relationships bloom other than in fertile joint families?

Mother's wish for a fan must have come directly from her heart, because help came from unexpected sources. It was Rakshabandhan—the day dedicated to the everlasting love between brothers and sisters, where sisters tie rakhis (protected bracelets) on the wrists of brothers, and pray for their welfare. I returned home at the usual hour, around 11.30 p.m. Even mother was awake and I presumed that something was in the offing! In those days, the custom of nieces tying rakhis on their maternal uncles prevailed in the Marwadi community. Accordingly, mother had sent a rakhi and received a cash gift of

100 rupees from her maternal uncle, Jograj Gundharji, who lived in a small hamlet named Belwa Ranaji in Rajasthan. However, mother had other ideas about using the money rather than on herself, 'Bhavru, you better buy a nice fan with this money. The heat must be intolerable for you all.' Without any elaborate display of emotion, she placed the money in my hands. How easily she gave away something that was exclusively hers! I am sure she must have been elated by this precious gift sent by an uncle whom we otherwise had little contact with. Yet, she gave us that money unhesitatingly, without thinking twice. It was a mother's response to her own progeny's needs, how could she not rise to the occasion? Kantabai and I were dumbfounded by mother's act of grace. I would have been surprised if Kantabai did not shed tears of gratitude and contentment that night.

This is a mother's love! She proved that night that she had ceased to be a mother-in-law to Kantabai.

Whenever friction occurs between mothers-in-law and daughters-in-law, why does bitterness prevail instead of memories of pleasant occasions that could help in diffusing the situation? Why does this relationship have to be one of the worst amongst all domestic bonds? If one Kantabai could hinge her relationship with her mother-in-law on pleasant incidents rather than on irritating ones, why can't the countless other Kantabais do so? After all, there is no dearth of such good-hearted women in Indian society. What is needed is the willingness to compromise a little—to let love replace hurt. After that night, I don't remember any major unpleasant incident that occurred between Kantabai and mother in the ensuing two decades of staying under one roof. As for minor skirmishes, they did not last more than a couple of hours anyway!

A small table fan did find its pride of place in our room, and it served the mother and child very well for several years.

That fan manifested a lifelong cordial and respectful association with Jograj Gundharji's family. Even after my mother's demise, Kantabai maintained cordial relations with that family that strengthened with time. It is amazing how a small table fan can establish larger-than-life relationships!

Jograjji passed away within a year of that incident. But the fan, while cooling us, kept fond memories of him alive in our minds for years.

Drought is an intrinsic part of people's lives in perennially rain-starved Rajasthan. At the most there is one wet monsoon every three years. There were 10 to 12 inches of rain that year, which was the mean average. Around 1972, the marriage of Jograjji's daughter was finalized. Both my parents were keen to attend the ceremony. However, bearing in mind father's advanced age I was worried whether he would be able to cope with the rigours of a long journey. Ultimately, I conceded and started preparing for their travel. On returning from the wedding, mother started insisting that Jograjji's son, Bhikamchand, join me in my business.

Fortunately, the business was growing rapidly. I did not have my own shop yet, but I managed to operate from a friend or relative's premise. My parent company, Esso, was happy with my performance and had allotted me one more petrol pump and an agency for domestic cooking gas. Additionally, I had also started selling crude oil along with kerosene, petrol and diesel. In those days, electricity was a rarity in rural India. Hence, the farmers used to depend largely on oil engines for irrigation and other requirements, and those engines were fuelled by crude oil. Naturally my business got a major fillip with this new activity.

When I returned home one day, mother said, 'There is a letter from Bhikamchand, Jograjji's son. What if we invite him to join your business? It will give him decent employment, and you will also get a trusted family member to look after your business.'

Bhikamchandji or Bhiku mama joined my business in 1972. Kantabai and I felt extremely happy that we could do something for Jograjji's son. We had not forgotten those swelteringly hot nights when the table fan was our only comfort. When Bhiku mama settled in Jalgaon after marriage, Kantabai herself arranged for many of their domestic necessities. Although Bhiku mama and Tulsi mamiji were younger than us, they were our uncle and aunt in terms of relationship, and so we used to bow to them whenever we met! It is in the Indian cultural ethos to revere higher relationships, and as envoys of this cultural heritage, we felt heartened to touch their feet.

Many years later, Bhiku mama's son got married in 2007. The ceremony was held at Jain Hills (our corporate headquarters in Jalgaon) amidst much pomp and gaiety. I was invited to speak on the occasion before a large and distinguished gathering. In spite of ill health, I seized the opportunity to do so. I could not help vividly recounting the entire 'fan' episode—how, 45 years ago, a money order of 100 rupees and a fan bought with that money had taught us an invaluable lesson in gratitude. I was overcome by emotion while I spoke. I later learned that many in the audience had had similar experiences and many eyes were moist because of personal memories.

It is not necessary that only blood relations come to our help when we need it. Destiny is very strange indeed—sometimes total strangers descend into our lives and help us out. They are the Almighty's ambassadors, God's good helpers. Such noble people enter our lives at the most unexpected time, in the most unexpected way. I concluded my speech by acknowledging the strange ways of destiny that were beyond human comprehension.

I saluted the noble souls who had come into my life and enriched it with their magnanimous acts. There was my mother, there was her uncle, Jograjji, and now, there was Jograjji's third generation entering matrimony in front of my eyes. I spoke for nearly forty minutes and at the end of it, started feeling a little better. My eyes welled up with tears. My heart and mind also felt lighter. Perhaps, I had repaid, at least in part, Jograjji's debt.

This was an event that brought back many memories of my mother. I had learnt a lot from this event. I may never be able to repay in full the debt to my mother's maternal uncle; nevertheless looking at the couple on the wedding dais, I felt content that I was able to host their wedding and I am truly proud of Bhikamchandji and his highly educated son.

7

OUR RESIDENCE AT Tijori Gali was located on the first floor of Bhate Building. Two other families stayed below and across from us. Potable water was available on the ground floor for a limited time only. So Kantabai had got into the habit of standing in a queue and fetching two buckets every day from the ground floor. Other family members also did the same. During our stay there between 1954 and 1963, the house was always overpopulated. My father Hiralalji, my brother Kantilal and I, along with our families, and aunt Nathibai were the permanent occupants. Besides, my mother, Gaurabai, and uncle Bansibhau's wife, Tarabai, also used to come from Wakod for periodic visits. Later, Bansibhau's whole family settled in the same house after migrating to Jalgaon from Wakod. There was a time when the small house accommodated as many as sixteen people! At times, Shivrajji's wife when pregnant had to be brought to Jalgaon for her delivery. At such times, we had to temporarily rent an extra room somewhere nearby.

In short, this house was also a guest house. It was home to three full-fledged families, consisting of three generations, with a second home for a continuous flow of guests. Given the chaos, the three-sided verandah of 4'x4' was a welcome extension, not to mention the terrace, which doubled up as a sitting room-cum-bedroom at all times except during the peak monsoon months. It was an unwritten law that the female-folk slept in the kitchen, and the men occupied the verandah or terrace, depending on the season. In spite of such acute shortage of space, I was privileged to have a room to myself. I was the youngest and most pampered one around, and of course, recently married!

With this preferential treatment, a revelation dawned on me—it is all about creating space even when and where there is no space! 'Space' for me now became a powerful metaphor for the large-heartedness and the accommodative spirit of my family members. Space for me now gained a much larger context. It detached itself from the conventional understanding of a measurable floor area. Instead, it gained a new dimension of immeasurable mutual care and concern. When such a strong-willed spirit of sharing and caring exists in joint families, other mundane matters like the necessities and preferences of different members, their likes and dislikes, their personal penchants, planning and provision of resources get absorbed automatically into the family system. What is required is mutual coexistence, feelings of compassion and joint ownership of this purpose. Such an exalted purpose is born in a family only when individuals don't let narrow individualism come in the way of the collective good. Self-denial and sacrifice, when called for, must govern the ethos of a happy and harmonious joint family. The elders must possess smaller aspirations, and the young must think and act with the maturity of elders. If a joint family's ethos is rooted in reconciliation, and if its foundation is reinforced with compromise, there will always be enough 'space' for everybody's welfare. I must, however, concede that economic considerations were at the root of such a necessity. I must also hasten to add that such economic constraints cannot be the only basis of this glorious joint family tradition. The basis, if any, was compassion combined with the reality for an accelerated economic growth for every part of the family.

Voices and noises travelled fast from one corner of that

small house to the other, 'That scoundrel has looted me in every way—he has taken away my money, gold and silver, even my farmland and my cattle wealth! Now, what is left for me? He will bear the curse of a hapless widow.' Such troubled curses, incoherently uttered by a mentally challenged Rajkunwarbai echoed in the house one day. She had come from Tondapur and had been our guest for some time. After a while, sorrowful sobs followed these curses. Kantabai was busy in the kitchen. I had left early, saying that I would be in for dinner with some guests. My wife was happy to hear that; her habitually late husband would come home early and after the dinner meeting with the guests, the little ones will at least receive goodnight blessings from him. Lost in her own thoughts, she ignored Rajkunwarbai's mumblings.

My uncle Ranidanji considered Rajkunwarbai a sister. My father and my uncles Ranidanji and Bansibhau used to visit Tondapur for business often. In those days, the three Ranka brothers—Punamchandji, Takhatmalji and Jodhrajji were prominent Marwadi leaders of Tondapur. They had migrated there from Nagpur. The famous public ground of Nagpur, Kasturchand Park, is named after one of their relatives. All three of them were very principled Gandhians and enjoyed a high reputation in the town and the community. Rajkunwarbai was Takhatmalji's wife. She was from a Choradia family, and as the Choradias belonged to the same family lineage as ours, she was our guest whenever she visited Jalgaon and would consider all the male members in our family as her brothers.

It is said that I was born only after my parents had sought many divine favours. I was God's child, everybody's favourite. Rajkunwarbai was also very fond of me. She would not tire of singing my praises and foretelling my bright future, 'You people talk about one motor car but wait and see, my Bhavru will one day have four cars parked in front of the four gates of his mansion. We will need many sacks to stuff his daily earnings. God forbid, even if the entire world is doomed, my Bhavru will remain unscathed.' I was thus the apple of everybody's eyes.

It was customary for my uncles to carry a packed meal with them whenever they visited Tondapur for work. But the bighearted Rajkunwarbai would always insist that they discard the stale tiffin and eat a fresh, hot meal prepared by her. Time was not kind to her, and she became mentally affected. Kantabai was aware of this tragic background, and that is why she used to remain unperturbed by Rajkunwarbai's behaviour and language.

Kantabai often left our son Ashok in the care of Rajkunwarbai while she attended to her daily chores, so that the poor lady's ailing mind could get some constructive activity and she would forget her affliction. It was very sad to see Rajkunwarbai, an intelligent and dignified lady, in such a piteous condition. It is indeed true; your direction is always decided by your destiny. Fate, providence, destiny…call it what you may, its way of governance will always escape our limited intellectual capacity. Who can ever fathom what is in store for them tomorrow? Our destiny is not in our hands. But to face whatever is destined with grit and resilience is certainly in our hands. Kantabai had accepted both these realities. She never questioned what she faced; instead she utilized her energies in finding a solution to that situation. This attitude and this ability made Kantabai what she was.

The way Kantabai dealt with Rajkunwarbai is an ideal example of how reconciliation works wonders in keeping a joint family undivided. There was no need for her to put up with this mentally unstable lady and her tantrums, as she already had her hands full. Given her extremely difficult circumstances, liabilities like Rajkunwarbai could have been easily dispensed with. But she never shied away from anything that family obligations had imposed upon her and never complained while doing her duties. It was a different era and a different lot of people. People respected interrelationships; they endured them all the time. The resultant sacrifices, hard work, forbearance, all were accepted with a sense of contentment and happiness. That we are somewhat different—was a feeling that never showed up. Such people if they were there were there by exception. Good-neighbourliness, love for the village and even foster relationships were maintained as if they were close ones. Thus, all the things around had an air of purity. These were not just accepted but respected by most of the people. Most of all, it was a cultured, traditional joint family.

They genuinely believed that life is a yagna (a Vedic ritual where the fire is kept burning for all time, and sacrifices are made by each and everyone, be it royalty or commoners). Life is not designed only to fill one's belly, but has to be lived in harmony with others and all the five elements—earth, water, fire, wind and sky. That is what they believed in and that is how they lived.

Kantabai had come into one such traditional cultured family. It was now her family. It, therefore, followed that she would inherit, accept and respect all the traditions, conventions, relationships and every obligation of the family. She was the incumbent new homemaker. She was well educated, cultured and had effortlessly immersed herself in her new role.

Kantabai had willingly embraced this family with full awareness of her future role and responsibilities. Her adaption was therefore seamless. The rest fell in place with time. Since willingness was there, compliance followed.

The fact that Kantabai too hailed from a similar cultured family of high moral fibre, helped her a lot in adapting to our family. To begin with, both the families were large. She had eight uncles and six aunts on the paternal side. Her grandmother had conceived twenty-three times, and lived to be hundred years old. Her grandfather, Chunilalji, was a well-known Honorary Magistrate. I still remember his picture sitting proudly atop one of the canons in the Bijapur fort, which aptly symbolized his upright status. He was also the chairman of the District Council. The palatial house where he lived is still known as Chunilal Bungalow. Kantabai's father, Uttamchandji, had also inherited a regal presence and a generous heart. He was the chairman of the city's Marketing Committee. Kantabai had this high pedigree and cultural footprint. She had admirable qualities like tolerance, gratitude, an amiable and agreeable disposition. She was never argumentative and never entered into verbal spats with anyone and respected everybody. Besides, she was educated, and this only added to her maturity and adaptability.

Even though Kantabai hailed from a non-Marathi state and town like Bijapur, she did have some Marathi families as her neighbours. These families were Konkani Brahmins of cultured and well-educated Maharashtrian ancestry. Well-known persons from such families like Mrs Kumud Bapat and Mrs Sudha Kulkarni were close friends of Kantabai. Her spoken Marathi was pure, chaste, fluent and perhaps even ornamental.

Kantabai had done her Bachelor's degree from the Distance Learning Department of Shreemati Nathibai Damodar Thackersey Women's University (SNDT University) in 1958–59. Her major subjects were English, Economics and Home Science. She was the first woman to graduate in Bijapur's Marwadi community. A retired professor and known Gandhian freedom fighter, Shri Hanumant Achari, used to give her tuitions at home in English. In those days, Bijapur was one of the more neglected and socioeconomically backward regions of Karnataka state.

The Marwadi community residing there was naturally orthodox and rigid. It could not come to terms with one of its girls attempting to graduate. Good news travels slowly, bad news travels fast, and scandalous news travels fastest! All hell broke loose when the community leaders came to know of this conspiracy-in-the-offing; they marched straight to Kantabai's house.

The hurriedly convened Disciplinary Committee confronted Kantabai's father, Uttamchandji, with a spirited attack against her proposed graduation, 'Have you lost your mental balance to even contemplate such a move? Why are you hellbent on ruining the girl's life? Do you think she will ever find a good match in the community with the curse of graduation? It is no small offence for a girl in our community to graduate. The nose stud will be bigger than the nose! A tradition will be broken; it will set a contemptible example.'

The decibel levels kept rising as they continued, 'Just think, how you will ever wed your graduate daughter when even sons rarely graduate in our community? Kantabai must be aged around fifteen-sixteen now—come to your senses, take our advice, marry her off at the earliest. She will be a mother of a couple of children in the time that she would take to finish college. Why are you bent on inviting trouble?' Lessons in worldly-wisdom, though entirely unasked for, were being showered on Uttamchandji.

Kantabai was her father's favourite. The gentleman was straightforward and progressive-minded. He adored his little angel—slim and fair, playful and bubbly, two pigtails tied neatly, and dressed in a ghagra-choli (traditional two-piece Indian attire). He was determined to give her the best education, notwithstanding the vociferous protests. He thought of a solution—he sent Kantabai to his elder daughter Shantabai's home in Bombay to attend extra classes for two months.

Our community has maintained a disdainful and perpetual disregard for education. An age-old Marwadi adage sums it up aptly, 'A literate person spends his life in service of the illiterate [but accomplished] person'. The underlying sentiment is that minds moulded just by academics, remain incomplete! Bookish knowledge is far inferior to practical knowledge and wisdom gained in a hands-on environment. This outlook prevailed over education per se, not just for girls' education.

Kantabai did graduate in 1959, despite all adversity. Her father was overjoyed and gave her some money to buy sweets to celebrate. But Kantabai went and bought a dhoti (a single unstitched Indian garment worn around the waist by men) for her father! I came to know about this from her sister Shantabai; my wife would never say anything in self-praise.

8

KANTABAI WAS RESTIVE and uneasy since morning that day. She had even vomited a couple of times, but continued her chores, thinking that such inconveniences were expected as one neared the full term of carrying a baby. By noon, however, she started getting labour pains. As always, I was out on business. Mobile phones were not invented then, so I was untraceable. Kantabai managed to reach Dr Chandrika Desai's maternity home in a horse-drawn buggy along with my mother. My father dispatched a small army led by my younger brother Kantilal to look for me. They remained unsuccessful even after searching for over an hour, and finally camped at the shop of B.M. Jain, which was my 'headquarters' then. In the absence of my own office and a telephone, I used to use his shop as my office. They rightly thought that I would come there sooner or later. At that point in time, I was busy with the Pearl-Yamaha representatives with whom I was conducting talks for their agency.

Kantabai delivered our second son Anil on 10 March 1965. I came to know about it around nine that night when I reached B.M. Jain's shop, and rushed immediately to the clinic along with Kantilal.

I knew that Dr Chandrikabai would be very unhappy that I was absent at the time of delivery. She refused to allow me to even have a glimpse into Kantabai's room, and instead beckoned me to her chamber. As I crept in, she began her well-intended, sarcastic admonishments. 'Welcome Mr Bhavarlalji the Great, it is such an honour! And you are so kind and considerate to have visited your wife on the same day of her delivering your second son. On the last occasion, you kept her waiting for five long days! Tell me Mr Businessman, do you think women are mere cattle? Don't you think they are human and they too have a heart, feelings and expectations? In spite of being in town, you were not beside Kantabai when she needed you the most. Can you comprehend how hurt and neglected she must have felt? She is an educated, thinking woman, and what would she have thought of you? Anyway, you are pardoned on grounds of compassion this last time. No excuses next time. Now celebrate. You have a son.' Her reprimand was well justified, and well meaning.

When a woman delivers a baby, she brings two new lives on earth—one for the baby and one for herself. The process is risky and prone with trouble. For the husband, to remain absent even during such a physically and emotionally trying occasion is certainly callous. I plead guilty, and wonder even today how Kantabai could have forgiven me for this unforgivable crime! She never ever complained about it to anybody, least of all to me.

That was Kantabai—the purest of pure souls. I felt as though I was reduced to a mere mortal in front of her divinity.

As the day of discharge from the clinic neared, my anxiety grew. There was simply no room to accommodate even the bare minimum needs of a new mother and a newborn baby in our two rooms. It already had sixteen or seventeen occupants. In those days, both the mother and child were kept in a separate room for some time after coming home. But where was that extra room? To add to our anxiety, Shivrajji's wife was pregnant again, so provision for her stay had also to be made in our home. And undoubtedly, there would be a steady stream of the usual visitors. I talked to mother. She thought for a while and came up with a solution, 'There is some room in Girdhari's home.'

Girdhari was my paternal cousin. He was a lecturer at the Polytechnic College. He had a rented three-room apartment on the third floor of Vadjikar Building. If one discounts the inconvenience of the third floor, the rooms were otherwise airy and spacious. Both Girdhari and his wife readily agreed to accommodate Kantabai in their home. It was a welcome relief for me. Those were early days yet; my business was small and my responsibilities were big. I had a modest turnover of 30–40 lakh rupees (around 55,000 US dollars in 2012), and a paltry annual earnings of around 45,000 rupees (around 825 US dollars in 2012).

There was space in Girdhari's home, but more importantly, there was space in his heart. This is how 'space' was created in those days, and somehow, life accommodated itself within it.

In today's nuclear families, the space in the homes is getting inversely proportional to the space in the hearts. Which modern and progressive family would ever think of helping a cousin who was apparently in trouble of his own making? Wouldn't it invade the private 'space' of the family? The egoistic, envious, indulgent, gloating, self-glorifying and self-centred environment of a nuclear family leaves no room for such exalted considerations that nurture joint families. They would prefer death to asking for help from family. And as regards helping someone in the extended family, the thought would be awkward and out-of-place at best, outrageous at worst. There is no entry for such thoughts in the single-track mindsets of modern families. They are accomplished and successful, and they are very possessive about their hard-earned success. They don't think anybody else has a right to their spoils. But in our time, success was considered a collective achievement and, therefore, its fruits were shared. We were interdependent and happy, not independent and alienated.

So much has changed in half-a-century! Have people changed with time, or vice versa?

Anyway, I promptly accepted Girdhari's invitation. And shedding the guilt complex of not having been by Kantabai's side when Anil was born, I focused on work with renewed vigour.

9

'YOU CAN DO so over my dead body, Mr Cherian.'

The loud agitated words were uttered by Munawar Baig. He was the supervisory officer of Esso Company's Jalgaon office, and Mr Cherian, at the other end of the phone, was the head of the company's Indore regional office. Mr Baig was in a rage, and had banged the phone down with that last sentence. He had done this to Mr Cherian, his immediate boss. The consequences could be devastating; he could be fired unceremoniously for this indiscipline. Getting a job in a reputed multinational like Esso was as meritorious as it was difficult. The company had a rigorous and stringent recruitment process. Given the situation, Mr Baig had placed his future in jeopardy with this impulsive outburst of emotion. Being a mute witness to this scene, I sat there petrified.

Mr Baig was an upright man of impeccable moral standards. Mr Cherian, too, enjoyed a high reputation as an efficient and successful officer. I was responsible, albeit indirectly, for this verbal spat. That is why my position was embarrassing and guilt-ridden.

In those days, the foreign oil companies used to import crude oil from India and refine it in their home countries, then bring back the finished products like kerosene, diesel and petrol for sale in the host countries. There was a governmental rider to this arrangement—the more the companies sold finished goods, the more crude oil they could import for processing. Although the profit margins were wafer-thin on finished products, the big money was on imported crude. Hence, there was fierce competition among the oil companies, including Esso, Burma Shell, Caltex, to sell maximum finished products, so that they could qualify for proportionately higher crude imports. These companies used to periodically devise various marketing schemes to motivate their agents to increase the sale of finished products.

We (Jain Brothers) were Esso's agents. Mr Cherian had told Mr Baig that if he was able to sell 2 lakh litres of kerosene between April and June in the Jalgaon region, Mr Cherian would issue a special credit note of 5 lakh rupees as bonus. The target was met. Jain Brothers had sold 70 per cent of that quota, and as such were eligible to get 70 per cent of the bonus money. However, apparently the commitment had slipped Mr Cherian's mind. When Mr Baig called him to issue a credit note of three lakh fifty thousand rupees in our name, he replied curtly, 'No credit note can be issued to your dealer Jain Brothers.' Perhaps it was Mr Cherian's cursory manner and conclusive tone that had made Mr Baig blow up, 'You cannot go back on your word, and if you want to, then you can do so over my dead body.' The unseemly incident had occurred in the office of the Nandurbar distributor of Esso. Mr Roshanbhai and I were witness to it. I felt deeply disturbed. Mr Cherian could unceremoniously dismiss our claim for the bonus. Mr Baig could be in trouble because of his forthrightness. And I could be in trouble, too, if we did not get the said bonus. So much was at stake.

Jain Brothers had reached a turnover of 56 lakhs by then, with a net profit of around 2 lakhs. Yet, our situation was still hand-to-mouth and the bonus amount could make or break us. Hence, the matter acquired life-or-death proportions for me. If we did get the bonus, it could facilitate additional business that would increase our clear profit by around 2 or 2.5 lakhs rupees by the year-end. On the domestic front, we could usher in better days, what with the recurring expenses of a household of ten members, children's education and other mounting costs. There were also outstanding dues on account of my younger brother Kantilal's recent marriage. Finally, I badly needed a shop for my growing business, and to switch over from my ancient Luna moped to a motorcycle or a car.

The immense pleasure that hard working people derive from hard-earned money is comparable to the delight that a starving person gets from the sight of a feast. Only people who give importance to love of labour will understand this sentiment. There is a vast difference, as vast as the space between the earth and the sky, between these two motives for earning: To earn to fulfill one's optimum requirements, and to earn to compound profits manifold and to thus amass disproportionate wealth. Our school of thought may be old, but old is gold! We were content with whatever we earned with our toil and sweat. We could sleep soundly after a day of hard and honest labour. There was no greed and no hurry to become rich. There was consideration and compassion for others in the way we did business. We did not want to become wealthy overnight. We looked forward to another day of hard and honest work every night. We earned to sustain and to help sustain. Isn't that the crux of the fashionable contemporary term 'sustainable wealth creation'?

The ways and means of earning money have become 'easy'. The importance, nay, the necessity of toil has been reduced. Smart work is now looking down upon hard work! I say, the amount of effort to be put in to earn have not reduced, only the nature of those efforts has changed. Mental stress and tension has replaced physical toil. Is it a good bargain? The same nature and amount of work which I used to do single-handedly, now requires full-time engagement of my four sons as well as my brother's son and countless other people. Do I derive the same joy and contentment from smart work that I used to get from hard work? The honest answer is 'No'. Anyway, that is the way things are! Let God's will prevail.

However, I do not want to sound hopelessly orthodox. We have to flow with the current, adapt to the changing times. In doing so, we have to strike a balance with the 'smart' and 'easy' ways of earning money. We may earn more and we may do so more easily. Subsequently, we will also spend more for the community and for the society, so that our core objective of 'sustain and help sustain' keeps thriving in letter and in spirit.

I do want to say this to today's white-collar city dwellers: A business culture based on the positive energy of love of labour is unparalleled. Try it just once. Walk your way to the office instead of commuting by any mechanized means one morning, and see the qualitative difference in your work for yourself.

Kantabai went into labour around midnight on 2 July 1966. Leaving Ashok and Anil in the care of her new sister-in-law Shantabai, she and mother left for Dr Chandrikabai's maternity home in a horse buggy. Simultaneously, the hunt for me began. I was holed up in Nandurbar, pursuing the matter of the bonus credit note. This was the third time I would be absent when Kantabai delivered—a dubious record of sorts. However, this time around, my advocate's mind had thought out an argument—the time of delivery is never predetermined, so how could someone like me who was fighting single-handedly on many fronts sit idle at home, twiddling his thumbs, waiting for the right moment. If the time of delivery could be predetermined, and I remained absent even after that, then I would accept my fault. However, even I knew that I was just finding excuses to come to terms with my guilty conscience. How I wish mobile phone technology had been invented earlier!

I got the news late at night in Nandurbar and immediately left for Jalgaon with Mr Baig, in his car. As the first rays of the sun kissed the earth, I entered Dr Chandrikabai's clinic.

Our third son was born at 3.37 am, and I was there by morning! Not bad, according to Dr Chandrikabai. She recollected that for Ashok's birth, I was late by five days and for Anil's birth, by five hours. Hence, my late arrival by just a couple of hours this time was almost forgivable. She chuckled, 'What more can be expected from a Marwadi businessman, for whom money is the ultimate goal of life! Business must get priority over secondary matters like births and deaths!'

Dr Chandrikabai had become a family member by then. Both the families had grown quite close between 1970 and 1980, and it had become customary to meet a couple of times a week for friendly, laid-back evening chats either in the compound of Khandesh Mills or at her residence. Even the Esso officials liked these relaxed, informal get-togethers, so they often joined the group. In this manner, the acquaintance with Dr Chandrikabai turned into a close friendship, which enabled frank and open-hearted debates on any subject. It was because of this openness that the noble lady-doctor used to narrate the details of Kantabai's deliveries to me.

I knocked and entered Kantabai's room, and the relatives and nieces erupted in a joyous chorus, 'Bhau, congratulations and celebrations!' A third son was born, which was a rare triple-luck! The mother gained instant celebrity status. Although this was indeed an occasion of tremendous joy for me, I could not help musing on Indian culture's obsession with the male child. My role in the birth-process of our sons was limited to just sowing the seed. Only two entities have been gifted with the power to procreate—mother earth and the mother. All other 'creations' are artificial manifestations or making deals with nature or her elements. Yet, we look down upon the birth of a girl child, one of the only two procreators!

Basking in the glory of having given birth to yet another life, Kantabai was filled with contentment and pride. All others left the room one by one as I entered. We spent over an hour in intimate togetherness. The glow of new motherhood had enveloped Kantabai's face. Profound, selfless and mutual gratitude filled the room as I went closer to her. We smiled at each other, a smile full of the anticipation and excitement that is exclusive to parents meeting for the first time after the birth of their child. That quality is impossible in any other type of smile. The most profound similes and metaphors of any language could never adequately express the pristine purity of that smile. In moments like this silence is sweet. We sat there just like that, silently drinking in the moment, letting mutual joy and satisfaction sink in. After an eternity, I touched her tenderly. She was well aware of the language of my fingertips, which was by now restless to become the language of lips. Kantabai shied away for a fleeting moment, 'Please don't.' But I knew she meant, 'Please yes'. As our embrace became intense, the universe ceased to exist for us; we had just created one of our own. Not a word was spoken; there was no need to speak. When silence is golden, why break it with words? When speech becomes ineffectual, the potency of pure emotions takes over. Such purity is totally unpretentious, totally truthful, like a silent prayer that is too profound for words. Our embrace at that time had the quality of a prayer, uttered for our newborn baby. We named him Ajit—the unconquerable.

As we came out of the trance, I said in mock exclamation, 'But we always wanted a daughter!' Kantabai replied with her typical playful humour, 'And from where would a daughter emerge? You sow wheat, then how can you harvest bajra? How can my lame wish prevail over your weighty aspirations?'

I matched her wit with mine, 'And who is prevailing over whom now?'

'You are so impossible', Kantabai's cheeks reddened. She quickly hid her blushing face behind her sari.

Ajit was born early in the morning on 3 July. The quick succession with which good events occurred thereafter had us all astonished and overjoyed.

Mr Baig called up on 7 July, 'Mr Cherian has sent me your credit note of three lakh eighty thousand rupees. I am coming to give it to you, but I will charge my usual fee of a hearty home cooked meal.' I was speechless.

Mother burst out with joy, 'If the good news of Ajit's birth is worth its weight in gold, this bonus amount is worth its weight in platinum.' She added a hearty rejoinder, 'It is all due to the auspicious entry of Ajit in our home. My bahu (daughter-in-law) is good luck personified. She has borne us three jewels. There can be no equal to our Kantabai in the whole town.'

Mother's joy knew no bounds. She had witnessed eight of her children die before her own eyes. For her, the joy of nurturing three grandsons was immeasurable. She exclaimed, 'My longevity has been increased by a decade.'

As mother rejoiced, my mind was harbouring a totally different thought—what if three daughters were born to us instead of three sons? Would mother still be so ecstatic? It is one of the most tragic paradoxes of the Indian social setup that in spite of being women and mothers themselves, Indian women feel burdened, unfortunate, lesser in motherhood, and even jinxed when they give birth to a girl child. The taboo is laced with heartbreaking irony. It pains me immensely to see this unholy belief being passed on from one generation to the next, by none other than mothers to their daughters.

The horrendous cases of abortion of female foetuses are rising unabated in our society. The weight of this social crime becomes unbearable when statistics prove that such cases are most prevalent in the Jain community. To think that Jains, the apostles of peace and non-violence, also perpetrate such heinous violence in the wombs of Jain mothers. Kill life even before it is born? What sort of Jains are we? Do we even qualify to be human? To tolerate such a monstrous, hypocritical, pseudo-progressive society, even passively is an unforgivable crime against humanity.

10

THE BIG COMPOUND of Chunilal Bungalow in Bijapur with its dense foliage was home to many snakes and scorpions. Even in her childhood, Kantabai was fearless. She used to catch them with a pair of kitchen tongs and put them in an earthen pot. Thieves also often came to the house. Kantabai's sister, Shantabai, once told us of an incident where Kantabai had driven away a notorious thief all by herself.

The word 'fear' was perhaps nonexistent in Kantabai's dictionary. But this total lack of fear and the ever readiness to take on hazardous tasks impulsively, would sometimes invite avoidable accidents. Such misadventures can create lifelong physical injuries. My younger brother's wife, Shakuntalabai, told us that this is precisely what happened to Kantabai. It was the peak of the monsoon season. While returning from the death anniversary ritual of my uncle, Ravatmalji Desarda (Girdharilal's father), in Chahardi, Kantabai and the other ladies had to face the wrath of the swollen Paldhi River that had breached the small bridge spanning it. There was a long queue of vehicles stranded at both ends of the bridge. The adventurous, inventive mind of Kantabai went into overdrive, and she quickly came up with a solution. Inevitably, it was risky and hazardous, but full of enterprising spirit. It is only the outcome of such ventures that can label such impetuous behaviour as an 'adventure' or 'misadventure'.

Kantabai proposed, 'Let us ladies form a human chain and with our combined strength, cross the bridge.'

The water on the surface was deceptively calm. It had a very strong undercurrent, and it was at its fiercest in the mid-portion.

Kantabai gauged the danger and cautioned everybody, 'Be steady and walk slowly with firm feet.' But the one who had forewarned became the victim of her warning! Kantabai stepped on a sharp stone and immediately faltered. She had sprained her leg, and sharp pangs of pain started shooting up from the injury. With a strong will and firm resolve not to break the link in the human chain, she somehow managed to cross the bridge with the other ladies. But by then, the pain had become excruciating.

Nevertheless, she tried to sound composed, 'I will just attend to my leg.' She tried to doctor the severely sprained, bent leg by straightening it forcibly with her hands. These amateur ministrations to the injured leg only worsened her condition.

No doubt, courage and guts are essential in life, and especially in overcoming unforeseen situations. But hasty and unpremeditated actions taken without proper assessment of their outcome can land one in lifelong trouble. After that incident of 'self-help', Kantabai was never able to walk straight with an erect stride. Her leg impairment and the resulting pain became chronic and lifelong.

Notwithstanding the negative outcome of this tragic incident, Kantabai's brave nature, innate ability to take risks and positivity became my undying sources of inspiration even in the face of herculean hardships.

But...but today was a different situation. Kantabai was admitted into Dr Chandrika Desai's clinic for the delivery of our fourth child. The doctor and her husband were closely monitoring her condition. However, the situation turned critical soon after delivery. During sterilization, it was found that Kantabai urgently required a hernia surgery. Worse, it had to be performed immediately. Dr Desai thought of calling Dr Bendale, who was a renowned surgeon in Jalgaon in those days. The clinic was just behind Dr Desai's hospital, and he was easily accessible.

Breaking my previous records, I was present at the hospital at the time of childbirth. In fact, I had been at Kantabai's side when she was admitted to the clinic. Dr Desai took my consent, and Dr Bendale was called immediately for the hernia surgery. The procedure caused great blood loss because of the large quantity of fat that had to be taken out. Kantabai's condition was becoming more critical with each passing minute. I was called in and the gravity of the situation was explained. I got extremely tense, with all sorts of ominous thoughts and premonitions invading my mind. Kantabai needed blood very badly and very urgently. She was almost comatose. Looking at her averted and expressionless face, it seemed as if she had turned her face away from us!

The situation rapidly deteriorated into a medical emergency. I was shaken to the core and disoriented. We were all clueless as to how and from where to procure the A+ blood that Kantabai required so urgently. Everybody started running around in different directions, frantically exploring whatever sources they could think of to procure blood. With great difficulty we managed to get one bottle. But it was simply too little! Our entire family did not have a single member who belonged to the A+ blood group! And the search for blood from elsewhere had been unproductive so far. I was at my wit's end, appalled by the rapidly worsening situation, and the magnitude of the possible consequences. Yet, utterly helpless by the situation. Kantabai's condition also seemed to be deteriorating very fast. My frustration was taking the form of red-hot rage.

How could such a renowned, expert and experienced

surgeon overlook one of the most critical requirements of an emergency operation—that there was enough blood available! Especially when the case was very complicated and it was a matter of life and death. This was really deplorable in a surgery of this kind. I felt proper planning was not done. The problem was that the question of blood supply had been overlooked in the scramble to perform the operation on time. My anger knew no bounds, but I somehow composed myself. Kantabai was still critical, lying unconscious on the operating table. Two more bottles of blood were needed immediately.

I needed something or someone to soothe me and raise my shattered spirits. Even in her semi-conscious state, Kantabai could perhaps gauge the need to support me. Overcoming all her pain and suffering, she made a supreme effort to open her eyes. She mustered up all the strength that still remained in her weakened body and gestured for me to come closer. Her lips quivered and she mumbled a few barely audible words. I bent to listen to her, and what I heard made me love her all the more at that moment. She made me feel proud to be her soulmate.

'Now look here my love, stop worrying, will you? As long as you are with me, nothing can happen to me. Just hold my hand. Let me feel your strength seep into me. So what if our blood groups are different? Let your love flow into me freely, and I will survive this calamity, I will live. That's a promise. Don't you dare think I am going to let go of you so easily. We have miles to go still. Our dreams are yet unrealized. We have four angelic sons by our side. Have faith in your Kanta, she won't desert you.'

Exhausted by the strain of speaking, Kantabai slipped back into semi-consciousness. But the promise was made, and it was enough for me to gather myself together. My brave Kanta could play with snakes and drive out dreaded burglars, so how could even this significant calamity measure up to her indomitable spirit? Besides, her resilience was 'seasoned' by the hardships and the trying conditions of our domestic life. In that profound moment of self-realization, I knew how strong she was and how weak I was. I did not know whether to smile or to cry.

I felt momentarily safe. But my eyes would not dry; the shock was very deep. My life was falling apart.

The pain of departing is felt more by the one who is left behind. Even the thought of losing Kantabai was unthinkable for me. I was numb with grief. I simply could not imagine life without her or life after her. In a delirious state, I kept talking to myself and consoling myself. I invented a nice, soothing thought; both Kantabai's mother and grandmother were still alive. So, it was in her robust genes to live long. Kantabai will make it. She has to.

Thanks to the prayers and Kantabai's own resolve, providence came to our rescue. After a while, two associates from the company came and gave their blood. They were God-sent. The Almighty had finally heeded our pleas. The operation was finally completed, after hours of nerve-racking anxiety.

This crisis brought back memories of another recent accident which I had faced just a few months before Kantabai's fourth delivery. It was around two in the afternoon. I had left my Shivaji Nagar petrol pump to come home for lunch in my Ambassador car. Suddenly, a small boy who wanted to cross the road rushed in from the left. I was driving in the middle of the road. The distance between the boy and my car was hardly six feet. I blew the horn repeatedly and jammed the brakes, but the boy was so petrified that he was unable to decide which way to go. He started running back towards the left. I veered the car sharply towards the right, and banged into a lamppost. The impact was so strong that the iron pole bent from the middle.

It is now forty years since the incident and the bent pole still stands in its place, a mute testimony to the accident. The car had banged into it so hard that I was forcefully pushed forward. Luckily, the front seat had slid back with the impact and my chest was saved from hitting the steering wheel. However, I was unconscious for a short time due to the trauma. People from the Kanji Shivji Mill from across the road came running and carried me to their office. Soon, the news spread all over Jalgaon. My uncle Dalubhau was in town that day and was going somewhere for work. On getting the news, he immediately rushed over to me, riding a borrowed bicycle; he must have ridden one after three decades! The news was also conveyed home.

A pregnant Kantabai was shocked on hearing about the accident. Such news can adversely affect the would-be mother's condition and can even cause a miscarriage. However, fortunately, no harm came to Kantabai or to the unborn baby. I, too, was unscathed, and that was enough for her to gather her composure quickly. Both having survived potentially fatal calamities, we had got a new lease of our lives. It is my firm conviction that such miraculous escapes are indeed made possible by the sheer strength of one's true love for the other. It is indeed difficult to say whose good luck saved me, but I would like to think that it was Kantabai's luck that acted as my saviour.

Our fourth son Atul was born on 6 January 1969 at 9:41 pm. He was a merry little fellow, oblivious of all the frantic happenings just after his birth. Kantabai opened her eyes at around 2 in the morning and immediately inquired, 'Where is my baby?' She was told in detail about the nerve-racking developments that had taken place since she had slipped into unconsciousness after talking to me. My mother and other women in the family were attending to the baby, and Kantabai was assured that there was no need to worry now; the worst was over. In fact, everybody was more concerned about her frail condition than that of the hale and hearty baby. Kantabai looked weak and pale, all her energy having been totally sapped by the near-fatal incident. Looking at her, I now actually experienced what I had merely thought about at the time of the birth of our first son, Ashok—when a woman gives birth, she actually brings two lives on to this earth; the baby's and her own!

What one gets after extraordinary difficulties and hardships, becomes all the more precious and loved. Was this the reason for Atul being his mother's most beloved son? Or was it because he was the youngest? She would dote on him day and night. She would keep him close to her heart all the time. Her adoration grew as Atul grew older. When he was studying in college in Pune, she would fret and fuss if there was the slightest delay in communication between them. She would long to hear his voice, as a cow would to get a glimpse of her wayward calf.

11

REFLECTING OVER THE crisis, my thoughts went back in time. Was it the correct decision to opt for children in the first ten years of our married life? The four births were spaced out with a gap of a little more than two years between them. Will giving birth in such quick succession have a lifelong effect on Kantabai's health? Will this create inherent problems in our last two children's growth and development? And will sterilization create any long-term side effects for Kantabai? I feared that our decision, which was based purely on logic and future planning, and which had not considered any health-related aspects, would prove to be wrong in the future. But then, it was a different era when such subjects were not discussed with today's openness. I should definitely have taken medical advice on this matter, but I must admit that I was full of inhibitions to discuss a subject like this.

A decision taken ten years ago was now weighing me down with the burden of its moral accountability. For its possible folly! It could have grave consequences on Kantabai and on the children. God forbid! What if it resulted in something dreadful? What would my children's and my future be if something happened to Kantabai? Was I blind to the fact that Kantabai was putting on weight after every delivery and that her abdomen was loosing elasticity? I overlooked it all and conveniently presumed that it was a hereditary trait. But in that moment of reflection and repentance, I finally came around to accepting that her physical deterioration was due to the quick succession of the four childbirths. They were planned to suit an ambitious man's career goals, not a woman's health.

I was guilt-ridden, entangled in the web of painful thoughts. Kantabai's image before me was hazy with the misty film that blurred my eyes. My family, relatives, friends and well-wishers were all there, but their consoling could not dam the flood of tears rolling down. They themselves were so distraught that they needed moral support just as much as I did. They were extremely worried about the outcome of this crisis. They kept looking in the direction of the operation theatre all the time to hear some good news. Brother Kantilal, uncle Dalubhau and approximately forty to fifty relatives and friends waited in the hospital premises. Some eyes were wet like mine, while some others were shut tightly in earnest prayer.

Emotions were fluctuating between anguish and anxiety. The tension was invisible but palpable, like a blanket of fog that covered our cold, numb hearts. Just then, Dr Chandrika Desai emerged from the operation theatre and announced, 'Both the operations have been completed successfully. Kantabai is in no danger now.' A big wave of relief swept over all of us instantly. The faces lit up with joy and everybody breathed easy.

I was satisfied that the operations were successful, but the shadow play of contrasting thoughts and emotions continued in my troubled heart. I was restless to see my newborn angel; my eyes were pining for the first glimpse of him. Slowly, I approached his cradle. He was indeed hale and hearty. Seeing him in a fine condition, I, too, forgot all worries for a moment. But soon, a worrying thought gnawed at my heart; will Kantabai be able to breast-feed him? She looked so weak and anaemic.

A mother's first milk is like the first showers that drench the starving, parched soil. There is no substitute to mother's milk on this earth. No vitamin, tonic or enzyme can ever replicate its wholesome goodness. It is the elixir of life which nurtures all life on earth. Oh God, let not Atul be deprived of this! Kantabai was indeed very feeble. Her hemoglobin had come down to nine from fourteen. The unforeseen and unprecedented medical emergencies had caused further rapid deterioration in her condition. I was constantly surrounded by negative thoughts and I blamed it all on myself.

At the same time, I was also aware that it was our joint decision to conclude the child-bearing stage in the first decade of our marriage. It was taken with a view to dedicate the rest of our lives to their ideal and healthy upbringing. No doubt, this thinking had its own logical high ground. It was very much a part of our broader view that all planning and provision for our children must be over before we leave this earth.

From a practical and professional angle, it is always advisable that our children become self-sufficient while we are around. Such a plan should be preferred any day. If ever they face major challenges or problems in life, we should be there to provide moral and material support. Our joint decision was taken after taking into consideration such a far-sighted view. Kantabai had never ever questioned this decision, leave aside opposed it. Given this background, where was the need for this guilt? I was consumed by conflicting and confusing thoughts that swayed my sense of judgment from one extreme to the other.

I also contemplated that during the same decade my career had progressed well. During the period of two years between Ajit and Atul's birth, my turnover had doubled to almost 1 crore rupees (2 million US dollars as per 2012 exchange rates). The profit had also doubled. Esso had allotted one more petrol pump to us in Savda village in Jalgaon district. We had also been given the agency for domestic gas supply in Dhule and a petrol pump in neighbouring Nagav, which were our first ventures outside Jalgaon district. My enthusiasm knew no bounds; it was as if I was on wings!

In appreciation of our outstanding performance in Jalgaon-Dhule districts in selling petroleum products (diesel, crude oil, lubricating oil, domestic gas, etc), Esso gave us seven more agencies. The dealership of Yamaha scooters gave us the added responsibility of expanding our operations all over Maharashtra. I was obsessed with meeting this challenge head-on.

My daily routine was full of contrasting roles; I was 'multitasking' on many fronts. On the one hand, I was engaged in hardcore rural marketing, which required native skills and tact, and on the other hand, I had to interact and entertain the sophisticated high officials of the parent company with urbane charm. There were no good restaurants in Jalgaon in those days. Hence, there was no option but to invite these officials home for lunch or dinner. That too, without prior intimation! However, Kantabai considered it her pleasure and privilege to welcome them with folded hands and sincere warmth. In India, a guest, particularly an unannounced guest is considered God, and Kantabai was hospitality personified for all these 'gods' whom I brought home at will.

True to her word, Kantabai had taken it upon herself to manage the kitchen with expertise. It can also be said that the 'always open' kitchen of our family had put Kantabai under its magic spell! Her friends had bestowed upon her the 'honorary' degree of Annapurna (Goddess who fills empty stomachs). And Kantabai had graciously accepted this second degree after her BA as a gift from her loved ones. South Indian dishes like dosa, vada, idli among others were very popular even in those days, and Kantabai was an expert in making these. That is why I used to ask lovingly as soon as I entered home, 'Where is the chef?' Even today all my sons miss her delicious dishes. They never tire of praising their mother's cooking to their wives! Sometimes this puts me in an awkward position at the dining table. However, I always side with the daughters-in-law, 'The dishes cooked by you all today are much tastier than Kantabai's preparations.' They would know that this was just my way of making them feel good, and would laugh it off in good humour.

To manage such a busy kitchen and its endless 'supply-chain', to cook for so many mouths almost single-handedly, to look after and care for the family and business guests, and to handle all other domestic responsibilities—Kantabai donned these many hats with gracious elan! Despite such mammoth responsibilities, she never compromised on the children's needs and cultural upbringing. Dalubhau's second marriage took place at that time. To top it all, the marriage of Kantilal, my brother, was also decided during the same hectic period. Although, she was the youngest, Kantabai did not shy away from accepting this major responsibility wholeheartedly.

This entire gamut of activities was efficiently managed without any problem within the limited 'space' of our two-room apartment. The constant flow of guests was also accommodated within the same 'space'. Yet, life was joyful and harmonious. There was never a hint of discord or disharmony, thanks to the large and kind heart of one fine lady that had enough 'space' for everybody in it.

I am proud of her not because she was my wife, but because she was 'Kantabai'. Every homemaker, even today, can be like Kantabai. And for sure, one comes across such industrious young women in society even today. It is not a question of changed times or changed priorities or changed lifestyles. It is a question of keeping a small part within us unchanged amidst all the changes that are happening around, so that happiness can grow and blossom within that small 'space'—just like it did in the olden days.

12

A PERSON WHO is passionate about achieving his goals never feels harassed or tired with work. To work, work and work continuously, without any fatigue, becomes his unchanging daily routine. Such a person is unstoppable in his journey; his motivation level is so high that it provides him all the energy he needs to work exceedingly hard. Even then, what if someone does succeed in stopping him? From experience, I can say that it is possible to stop even such an unstoppable person. However, the only one who can do it should be so close to his heart that he is not able to refuse him or her. For me, who else but Kantabai could do this?

'Listen, can't you postpone going to Bombay for a couple of days?' she entreated. Later, I heard Kantabai crying. I was puzzled and perplexed; what could be the matter?

It was so unlike Kantabai to stop me from my work. She had never posed nagging queries to me in our eight years of married life—questions which were commonplace in the lives of other couples. Such as, 'Where are you going?', 'When will you return?', 'You should have informed me earlier, now where is the time to even pack your bag?', 'From henceforth, do inform me before going anywhere,' etc. It is typical of women to do this, but Kantabai was an exception. That is why her sudden, uncharacteristic plea to postpone my work had me immediately worried. I reasoned to myself, it must certainly be a grave matter, or else Kantabai would never stop me like this. And her crying, confirmed it; she also looked very nervous and dejected.

Kantabai had still not quite recovered from the traumatic period of Atul's birth. The multiple surgeries which unfortunately had to be performed at that time—the childbirth, the removal of the uterus, removing the excess fat and the hernia operation—had left her physically and emotionally drained. Even though she never expressed it verbally, I was acutely aware of how much she needed my presence, my love and care to overcome this trying phase in her life. I could understand her condition and readily gave in. 'Okay, your wish is my command,' I quipped. But deep in my heart, there was a lurking sense of unease; could there be any other reason? She had never stopped me from my work before. In fact, she had gone out of her way to facilitate my working. Why this unusual request now?

I could have been inconsiderate and said, 'Please don't stop me', 'It is very important for me to go', 'Is your health not okay?', 'You always see me off smilingly, so what's the matter today?', 'You always sweeten my mouth with a piece of jaggery as a good omen to wish me a safe journey; why not today?' However, I thought it fit to quietly agree to her request. She seemed relieved and happy. All couples pass through such moments in their lives where silent agreement works better than spoken words. I was lost in thought, when the phone rang and I extended my hand to pick it up. Kantabai went in, wiping her tears. The tears of distress had now perhaps become tears of contentment and joy.

It was almost customary in those days for women never to hinder or stop men from going to work. The practice was all the more stringently applied to someone like me who was single-mindedly dedicated to work. Perhaps, it was heredity for me to think so and I also readily accept that it is not the best of practices. However, it was an unwritten dictum in our family never to obstruct men on their way to work and it was to be followed unquestioningly. Period. It had been observed since many generations, and it continues in the next generation even today.

My Bombay visit was important and critical in several ways. In addition to the agencies for domestic gas, kerosene, oil and diesel, Esso, the parent company, was about to award us a new centre for domestic gas in Malegaon in Nashik district. This was a momentous juncture in my career. The company followed a strict policy of not awarding more than one agency to any single dealer. However, we had been given eight! This was a rare exception made in the company's policy. A truly unique recognition of a dealer's exemplary performance.

The Malegaon agency had brought happy times to our family. The feeling of wellness and well-being had percolated into everybody's heart. The development, which had occurred after Atul's birth, was thought to have occurred 'because of Atul's birth'. He was the personification of a good omen. If the son was thus glorified, the mother acquired the status of a deity! My mother took it upon herself to lavishly praise both the mother and son to the entire town. The progress in business brought contentment and happiness to the family.

My business continued to grow by leaps and bounds. I now added auto spare parts, tyres, Escorts tractors, Rajdoot motorcycles, the agency of Adarsh Chemicals for Super Phosphate, and a petrol pump in Jalgaon city itself to my existing activities. It had now become inevitable to own business premises of our own. Companies like Escorts insisted that the dealer should own the showroom and servicing spaces. Hence, we thought of purchasing seven acres of land adjoining the MIDC (Maharashtra Industrial Development Corporation) area in Jalgaon. The deal was finalized at 6,000 rupees (around 110 US dollars as per 2012 exchange rates). But we did not have that much money in those days. We paid only 500 rupees upfront and sealed the deal.

13

IT IS TRUE that unforeseen problems strike just when you think that the worst is behind you and the path ahead is trouble-free. It seemed that I was inherently trouble-prone! Such problems strike you unexpectedly when you are off-guard, hampering your pace of work and marring your reputation. One can adopt a philosophical view and think that even the sun and the moon are not unblemished, so what is a mere mortal before destiny. One can even derive solace by thinking that in order to digest sweet success the sour juices of failure are required.

Rapid growth in business often invites such trouble in the form of jealousy, greed and cheating by your own people. Then, you become extremely wary and shaken. Your world turns topsy-turvy. You feel as if fate has hung you upside down from a tree!

A similar unforeseen development was responsible for that night's grim situation. I climbed down from the second floor of Ramesh Sadan and approached the waiting car. Two police officers and my advocate friend Mr UN Raisoni were already seated in it. Kantabai was standing beside the car with a tearful face. There was no jaggery to sweeten my mouth. Anguish was written all over her face. My entire joint family was also present there. I turned my face towards the east, closed my eyes and recited the Namaskar Mahamantra silently. I then turned to have a last look at my near and dear ones. Kantabai's eyes welled up with tears. She could not contain her pain, no matter how hard she tried. The recent developments had cast dark shadows of gloom. As it is, she had not yet fully recovered physically after

Atul's birth. The emotional stress only increased her distress.

An army of disturbing thoughts invaded my mind. The matter at hand was very serious, tricky and tragic. It could even turn out to be life-threatening. Not only our reputation, but our very existence was at stake. That night must have been filled with agony for Kantabai. She would have been tormented by the concern for my safe return. It was indeed a matter of life and death. A fleeting thought rushed through my mind; it was as if I was going to a dreadful war, the outcome of which was not in my hands. I then realized how difficult it must be for a soulmate to send her hero to war. Kantabai was looking at me unblinkingly. Was it because her eyes wanted to fill her heart with as much of me as possible?

However, she did not cry! My brave Kanta knew that her tears would shatter me; I would not be able to face the gravest trial of my life if she gave in to her grief. It must have demanded all her strength to keep her emotions in check. But she managed. Instead of tears of helplessness, a wave of positive energy arose from deep within her soul and through the windows of her sorrowful but resolute eyes, this energy travelled into me. Even today, I dread to think what would have been my plight had she broken down.

I was ready to leave. I looked straight into her eyes, seeking her permission as well as silently conveying to her that I will return victorious. She looked back in acknowledgment, 'Go safely, fight to win and return like a hero.'

I meant everything to her. I was her universe, and her entire existence revolved around me and the family. I too loved her totally and utterly. She was well aware that my absence would be sorely felt by my aged parents and others in the family. Her dedication and devotion made her put her emotions aside. She responded to the higher call of duty valiantly. Not only did she have to perform her own responsibilities, but she also had to make up for my absence and provide emotional succour to the family. 'We have to emerge unscathed from this crisis' became her mantra and mission.

I vividly remember every moment of that night even today. Before coming down to see me off, Kantabai had taken in the sight of the full household for a long moment, and then descended with a firm will and resolve. Were these our life's last moments of togetherness? 'NO', my inner voice screamed. Nothing of that sort will happen. Kantabai and her friend, Anjali Ajgaonkar, had even consulted an astrologer and he had predicted that we will all survive the crisis unharmed and unblemished. Kantabai was brimming with hope and confidence as she consoled me, 'I am with you till the end. I will not let anything happen to this paradise that we have created so painstakingly.'

As I stepped into the waiting car, I too became firm and told myself, 'The bugle is blown. Let us charge without worrying too much about the outcome. Kantabai is my inspiration.'

∽

'…Teach your family how to survive on paltry jowar rotis, because you, the breadwinner, are on your way to languishing in jail for a long, long time…' These words were from a threatening letter sent to me.

The 'author' had added, '…And you too get into the habit of using a grinding stone all day; that's what you will be doing in jail.' The author of this nasty letter was none other than Bhimraj Mothilal Jain (Kotecha), a helper in our office who had been promoted as an accountant.

Bhimraj was otherwise efficient in his work; he would sweep and clean the shop, tidy the gaddis (mattresses kept on the floor for sitting), and do all other mundane chores very well. However, looking at the rapid strides that Jain Brothers were making in business, greed overtook his integrity. He thought that he deserved more than his salary. He started eyeing a bigger piece of the pie. He worked with us for some time, and then stabbed us in the back. He managed to steal our accounts registers and important business documents, and headed straight to Ujjain in the dead of night.

Upon reaching Ujjain, he took refuge in the home of his brother-in-law Sharadchandra Mutha, who was a known income tax consultant of that city. He was widely rumored to be the right-hand man of the then central minister, PC Sethi.

'We are in possession of sensitive information about your business dealings. Our silence will cost you one lakh rupees. Pay up, or else…' Bhimraj started writing dozens of threatening letters to me from Ujjain, upping the ante of psychological warfare each time. The frightening thought of me going to jail and the family plunged into an economic and social abyss, as described in his last letter, shattered everybody's spirits. Its harsh tone and dire threat were indeed terrifying. That is why Kantabai was so justifiably distressed.

My success was hard-earned, a result of tremendous limitless toil and stress. I had earned every single rupee with the dint of sheer hard work. Our family's rocky boat, struggling to maintain its course in choppy seas all these years, was finally sailing in calm waters. With total transparency and fairness in my dealings, I had managed to build a good reputation for myself. I was emerging as a socially responsible, learned, knowledgeable and cultured entrepreneur in business and social circles. My family had also had a good foothold in the community and in society.

'…If I wish, I can wipe out your success in one stroke. Just one complaint to the income tax and other departments, and your shady deals and malpractices will be exposed. That one blow is enough to send you to jail.' 'I can straightaway send you to jail'. This intimidation sounded very real, since it now appeared that Bhimraj had done his 'homework' well before issuing me the threats. Knowingly or unknowingly, there were glaring disparities in our accounts and documents in the past few years. This may have happened due to too much work pressure and, as a result, the unintended oversight. This had been bothering us anyway. Now the situation was such that we could neither swallow nor throw up the bitter pill of insult and embarrassment resulting from this blackmailing incident.

Thinking that the best way to deal with a blackmailer is to avoid him, I had ignored all the threatening letters for the last two months or so. I had not answered a single letter. Seeing that his strategy of frightening me was not working, Bhimraj's frustration kept mounting. My strategy of provoking him with my absolute non-responsiveness finally led him to commit a critical mistake. The last letter that he had written amounted to extortion, theft of accounting records and threat of bodily harm. This was just the type of solid proof I was waiting for to build a strong case against him. My latent talent of an expert advocate came into play. I worked out a clever scheme.

I lodged a complaint in the Jalgaon city police station on 10 November 1969. The FIR (First Information Report) was lodged against Bhimraj Mothilal Kotecha and his brother, Rikhabdas Mothilal Kotecha, both from Jalgaon, and their brother-in-law, Sharadchandra Mutha, in Ujjain, under Clauses 215, 379 and 383 of the Indian Penal Code. The crime register of this FIR was 343. Bhimraj's nature of work in our office was mentioned in detail in the FIR. It was also mentioned that he had won our trust and confidence through his hard work, dedication and intelligence.

Thereafter, it was mentioned how, falling prey to greed, he had stolen our registers and important documents with the intention of blackmailing us. The FIR was backed by strong conclusive evidences. The case was airtight. The person who had stabbed us in our backs was trapped in his own web of greed. In order to strengthen the case further, I had attached photocopies of all the threatening letters that he had written to me.

When the police asked me, 'Where are the original copies of these letters?' I replied, 'I have returned them to Bhimraj. I had also sent 30,000 rupees along with those original letters, in denomination of 100s, as extortion demanded by him. I have also noted down the numbers of those 100-rupee notes.' I also attached this with the FIR.

The police inspector asked, 'You paid the money, but where are the registers and documents that would obviously have been returned upon receipt of the money?'

After listening to the entire story, he also wrote down my formal statement. I detailed in it how, initially, I had gone to Ujjain alone, and worked out the deal with Bhimraj and his brother-in-law, Sharadchandra. I also mentioned what happened to the documents after paying the extortion. I did not fail to add that the extortion money was paid by me under extreme duress. I also gave the names of all the people who were party to this conspiracy and extortion.

Rikhabdas, Bhimraj's brother, who was also living in Jalgaon, had visited my residence at Ramesh Sadan to convey Bhimraj's message of working out a compromise deal. In other words, he had approached me to say that he would keep quiet about the matter if certain sums were paid. I had recorded our conversation that took place at that time. It incorporated all the details of the entire episode. This piece of evidence made our case very sound. The police were convinced that it was a clear-cut case of cheating, forceful extortion, destruction of important proof, etc, and filed the complaint under appropriate clauses.

I then pressed upon them that the matter was grave and urgent, and it required immediate action. I even pulled some strings to compel the police to take instant action. The then deputy superintendent of police, Mr Pawar, and sub-inspector, Sawant, heeded my urgency.

This is how we left for Ujjain around ten that night. It was symbolic that our journey led us from darkness to light. We reached Ujjain's government guest house around five in the morning. We got down to work immediately after freshening up and left for Muthaji's house from where Bhimraj used to write those threatening letters to me and where our initial discussion to settle the matter had taken place. On the way, the police officers accompanying us, who were from Maharashtra, stopped at the Ujjain police station, which was in Madhya Pradesh, and formally informed them that they were here to investigate a case registered in Jalgaon, Maharashtra. They also asked for some local police support, but nobody was ready to join us at that early hour. Hence, we proceeded on our own to Muthaji's house where Bhimraj was staying.

'Who is there?' A middle-aged voice responded to the knock on the door.

Sawant replied, 'Police from Jalgaon. Open the door.'

The door opened after a couple of minutes. It was Mutha himself facing us. Seeing the police personnel and me, he gauged the situation instantly.

'What brings you here and whose authority do you have to disturb our household so early? I will not permit you in.' The reputed income tax advocate tried to prevail upon the situation, but in vain.

Sawant shot back in the typical authoritative and statesman-like tone of a Saraswat Brahmin (a high subcaste of Brahmins), 'We have registered a case against you in Jalgaon under sections 215, 379 and 383 of the Indian Penal Code. As an advocate, you would be well aware that under the provision of the Indian Constitution, I am authorized to go anywhere in India for search and seizure.'

Pawar and I were keenly watching the scene. It did not escape our attention that Mutha's son, who was standing behind him, was about to bolt.

Pawar immediately took out a revolver from its holster. He aimed it at the son and roared, 'Hands up! I will shoot without second warning if anybody tries to move.' Everybody froze.

The entire family was rounded up in a room. Pawar, Sawant and I searched all the five rooms, but could not find what we were looking for. We had started getting a little disheartened. Just then, we noticed a sixth room which was bolted from the outside. Pawar Saab opened the door. A woman was lying down in the room. She was writhing as if in pain.

Sawant asked Mutha's son, 'Ask her to get up.'

He replied, 'She is gravely ill.'

Pawar shot back, 'She doesn't seem to be so ill that she can't even sit up.' Muthaji then asked his wife to sit up, and she complied.

Pawar searched the entire room, but found nothing! Just then, his vigilant eyes noticed the pillow on which Muthaji's wife was sleeping. Surprise! The bag which we so desperately wanted was found hidden under the pillow. It contained the original threatening letters that Bhimraj had written to me. Both the police officers shouted in unison, 'We've got it!'

They were immensely relieved. Meanwhile, Muthaji was insisting on chai-pani (tea and refreshment), which is the metaphor in India to start the process of bribing to 'settle' the matter amicably. However, throwing cold water on his hopes, Sawant started writing the on-site report.

He asked sternly, 'Where is Bhimraj?'

Muthaji replied, 'We don't know.'

As providence would have it, Bhimraj made an entry just then. Sawant asked him about the 30,000 rupees.

He was shaken to the core, but managed to put up a brave front, 'We have not taken any money.'

Bhimraj was extremely edgy and frightened. Sawant searched him, but could seize just two 100 rupee notes from him. He tallied their numbers with the list that I had provided. Luck always favours the honest and the brave. He gave Pawar a high five and jumped joyfully, 'Arre, these numbers tally! We now have all the original documentary evidence and the stolen property'.

In most cases of theft of cash which are solved, it is 'claimed' by the police that the money was not recovered in full. Such claims may or may not be true. But in this case, I was present there and witness to how little was actually recovered. Moreover, the officers appeared to be honest. Even otherwise, money is like dirt on one's hands. It comes with the wind and goes with the water.

Wealth is a very funny kind of a possession. The more you get it, the more you feel that you have to have it. Money also defies the belief attached with it that it gives happiness and contentment. Actually, it gives us more pain than pleasure. And yet, the whole world is in a mad scramble for money! A person's mindset and money, both are known to create more problems than solutions to problems. But we foolish humans cling on to it.

On finding what we wanted, smiles returned to our faces.

We had succeeded in our mission. Sawant and Pawar started handcuffing the father-son duo. They were planning on parading the culprits through the streets of Ujjain with their hands cuffed. However, I could not bring myself to humiliate them so heartlessly. In a choked voice I urged the officers not to do this; what was the point in embarrassing them publicly?

I also requested both the officers, 'Sirs, Bhimraj and Mutha are enough for us to proceed with the case. I don't think the young son needs to be dragged into this battle. I am sure he will present himself to the authorities and give his full cooperation in the investigations as and when needed.' I was overwhelmed with emotion by then. I requested the officers to take them in our vehicle instead of walking them down the streets and they obliged.

We left for Jalgaon the way we had come. Our advocate, Mr Raisoni, and another gentleman, Mr Mohan Lodha of Pahur, who had also accompanied us, were waiting in the circuit house. We picked them up and proceeded for much-needed refreshments. Before returning to our waiting vehicle, I went to a telephone booth to call Kantabai to break the good news to her.

Back in Jalgaon, it had been a nerve-racking time for Kantabai. Her eyes were swollen from a tearful night of sleeplessness. But on hearing from me, her sorrowful tears transformed into joyful ones! She breathed easy after I narrated the happy ending to the incident.

Kantabai had never seen me doing anything negative. This was the first 'negative role' that she saw me play during our eight years of married life. She just could not believe that her husband could be so unyielding to anybody, even to the perpetrators of a premeditated, wrongful crime. It was as if she was exposed to a totally new dimension of my character that was in contrast to my image. Anticipating this beforehand, I had narrated the entire incident to her in toto before she could ask for details. She had no option, but to accept this tough side of her softhearted husband!

This was a one-of-a-kind incident in our married life. It provided an invaluable lesson, which, though painful, had its own value, both for a man who was on his way to enlightened entrepreneurship and the wife who was his unshakable strength and inspiration. A person whose positive energies were channelized totally towards purposeful and constructive work, a person who was possessed of an undying zeal to create something of lasting value for himself and for society—for him, to act in a negative and apparently vengeful manner was alien. His dilemma at that time is worth bearing in mind; shackled as he was by two chains of contrasting thoughts.

I had done my own share of soul-searching. Am I doing the right thing? Am I justified at all in taking this action that will ultimately harm someone? My religion, Jainism, commands me to forgive unconditionally. It is not up to me to be judgmental or to act punitively. Am I not playing God by being retributive? It is one of the fundamental tenets of the Jain religion to forgive and forget.

Most certainly, Bhimraj had contributed to my growing business. While working for us, he had been totally honest and sincere in his duties. Was it then morally correct to punish him the way I did? Whatever had to happen had happened. Was it not too harsh, even inhuman, to be instrumental in sending him to jail? And after all, who doesn't err on the moral or ethical side at some point or the other in life? He was after all a human being. He would have had his own compulsions that possibly led him to do what he did. After he had bolted with the account books, it may have been difficult for him to provide even two square meals a day for his children! It is quite possible that such a dire situation would have forced him to resort to this act. Nobody is a born wrongdoer. Nobody is a thief or a crook by choice. He may have committed this crime out of sheer compulsion.

On the one hand, my nobler side was promoting such exalted thoughts. At the same time, my pragmatic and worldly-wise, counter-thoughts screamed back at me, 'Nothing doing! The guilty must be punished. How else will society progress? If he is let off scot-free today, then the devil in him will get a free hand and tomorrow, he will become a compulsive crook. Cheating and blackmailing will become his second nature. He will become a threat to the society. The entire moral concept and legal provision of punishment is based on the thought of checking the culprit at the right time. There is a noble side to all punishments—it provides an opportunity to the wrongdoer to improve and to correct himself. Hence, by your actions, you are in fact giving Bhimraj an opportunity to realize his mistake and to correct himself. All penalties are inherently aimed at correcting the sin and providing an opportunity to improve oneself.

Besides, Bhimraj had dragged my family into this; my family who had had nothing to do with the entire unsavoury incident. It would have been okay had he limited his threats to me, but he had gone to the extent of intimidating my family, my wife and even my little sons. Further he had 'predicted' dreadful days of eating rotten grain rotis for my family. Even if one understands his crime, how could one forgive his inhuman action of dragging my innocent family members into this?

Anyway, it was pointless brooding too much on the incident. The arrow had already left the bow!

There is a very wise Marathi saying:

'Whatever deeds one is destined to do in this life, one is duty-bound to do, and bear the consequences thereof.'

How true these lines were, both for Bhimraj and for me!

I reconciled to reality, drawing from this wisdom. One more Hindi proverb helped me overcome my feelings of remorse:

'It can be forgiven if a human errs in observing his dharma (values), but, it is unforgivable if he errs in performing his karma (actions which he is duty-bound to perform).'

However, pain and anguish lingered within me for some time, as I had to perform this painful but inescapable karma. On the one hand, I was sorrowful at his plight. On the other, my anger had got the better of me.

14

THE AFTERNOON OF October 1965 was terribly hot. The household, at whose helm my mother sat, was buzzing with activity. Her wish was a loving command for everybody in the family. She had sent Kantabai and Rukmanibai to the bazaar, while she and Tarabai, Shivrajji's wife, were busy in the kitchen. She was cutting vegetables, while Tarabai was kneading the dough. Bansibhau's wife, also named Tarabai, was washing clothes and the dhab-dhab of wet clothes being beaten by a wooden club was resounding through the whole house. Little Sunita, the daughter of Shivraj and Tarabai, who was asleep, was probably disturbed by this noise. Everyone was preoccupied and no one noticed that she had woken up and crawled towards the sound. A glass filled with kerosene stood on top of the kerosene container in a corner of the room. The child thinking that it was water drank it. In just a few moments, she began convulsing with pain and started crying loudly. Panic struck the household, and everybody started running helter-skelter, not knowing what to do. Nobody had a clue about what had suddenly happened to Sunita.

Just then, Kantabai and Rukmanibai returned from the bazaar. Kantabai immediately took Sunita in her arms trying to comfort her. She retained her presence of mind under this grave emergency and pleaded with everybody to remain calm. One look at Sunita's clothes and the smell of kerosene emanating from them, and Kantabai immediately knew the problem. Without wasting even a second, she lifted Sunita in her arms and rushed to Dr Kotwal's clinic, which was located next door, opposite the bus stop. Since this was an accident and the patient was an infant, the doctor instructed her to go to the government hospital.

Kantabai took a tonga and reached the government hospital. Fortunately, Dr Jethmal Doshi was the medical superintendent there at that time and started the treatment immediately. A pipe was inserted into Sunita's abdomen and most of the kerosene was pumped out of the body. Medications were given as well. And soon, the child regained consciousness.

I was also informed of the accident. I was at our Shivaji Nagar petrol pump, discussing business with Mr Munawar Baig of Esso. On hearing the news, we immediately left for the government hospital, but by then, Sunita's condition was normal and the doctor said that she could be taken home. We all left in Mr Baig's car with Sunita sleeping peacefully on Kantabai's lap. Kantabai's presence of mind and timely action had saved the little angel's life.

There is a similar incident where Kantabai's innate ability to think clearly and act swiftly under emergencies saved the day. Our household in Wakod was full of guests of every age and gender spanning three generations who would come to spend the summer vacation there. Hastimalji, my uncle Dalubhau's father, who was paralytic, had also come. It was the mango season, and the children were having a mango-eating contest. One ripe, juicy mango was also offered to Hastimalji, who managed to suck and eat it, even though he was toothless. A second mango was offered, and then a third. However, this time, he swallowed the seed along with the pulp, and this got stuck in his food pipe. In seconds, Hastimalji started choking and gasping for air, his whole body convulsed with pain. The children panicked and ran to fetch Kantabai. She, who never even opened her mouth in front of elders, did not hesitate to take 'strong action'. She made a fist with her right hand like a boxer's and gave a few 'power-punches' on Hastimalji's back! She then forced him to bend over and out came the mango seed! Although everyone was horrified by her 'methods', they were certainly pleased with the outcome!

As I stroll down memory lane, one more incident flashes before me. When we used to live in Bhate Bhavan, little Sunita was in trouble again. The ladies were in a happy mood and getting ready to go to a movie. In the rush, Kantabai opened the wardrobe to take something out and then shut it hastily. Sunita's hand got caught in the door. She started crying and was inconsolable.

Although Kantabai was fearless, she was very kind-hearted as well. She could not help feeling guilty and responsible. She thought, 'If only I had not been so hasty, the little girl would have been spared this agony.' In repentance, for many years she did not see a single movie!

Sunita grew up to be Kantabai's favourite and the most beloved of all the little girls she had nurtured. She lived with us for eleven years, from 1977 when she was in the ninth standard through college and graduation, till her marriage in 1988. Her mentoring by her 'foster mother' was replete with good sanskaar; and a cultured, virtuous upbringing. Our reward for this was that we got to perform her kanyadaan, a part of the Indian marriage ritual in which the bride is given away to the groom by her parents with lavish gifts of clothes, jewellery and other precious items.

We all realize at some point in our lives that blood relations need not necessarily be the strongest or the most cherished of relationships. Destiny has its own strange yet wondrous ways of creating incredible relationships between strangers. Sometimes, people meet unexpectedly under conditions, either joyous or tragic, and the fond memories of that cherished togetherness create lifelong relationships. Likewise, intimacy born out of sharing joys and sorrows, help and support offered during times of need, deft and clever handling of a difficult situation in one's life by someone, a few words of comfort, even an understanding pat on the back can unite two hearts in an everlasting bond. Those who are sensitive to human needs and respect them, and those who believe in helping others, would value chance relationships as highly as bonds of blood or perhaps even more!

Today's families, who are largely under the influence of consumerism and have a self-centred mentality, may find my ideas old-fashioned and out of sync with their contemporary lifestyles. However, Kantabai and I have always cherished the relationships that were born out of being unconditionally good to others, without any self-interest. While doing whatever we could for others, the gratitude for the kindness received from them never left our hearts. That is why we always felt that everybody around us was 'ours'—that they were an inseparable part of our lives.

We always felt humbled when people genuinely respected us. At the same time, we never forgot that this respect came with inherent responsibilities towards our immediate joint family and the extended family consisting of all those around us.

God gave us four sons, not a single daughter. But Kantabai never ever regretted this. And why should she have done so? She always considered our relatives' daughters to be her own and brought them up in the best traditions of Indian values and culture. She mothered them with utmost love and care. Whether it was Rukmanibai's Sarla or Bansibhau's Chandrakala, she inculcated values in them. Later, Shivrajji's Sunita and Kantibhau's Anjali, too, were given the same love and care when they came to live with us.

Daughters are like full moons that light up our homes and hearts alike. When there are daughters adorning one's home, the attraction felt towards the family is indeed extraordinary. While Kantabai shaped these young, tender minds with the Indian perspective of ideal womanhood, she also taught them to live with dignity and self-respect.

Apart from the cultural, moral and ethical moulding, our 'daughters' also gained from the vibrant and energetic environment of our family. Our bustling household, always full of many guests from different walks of life, taught them invaluable lessons in pragmatism, tact, amiability, adaptability, presentability, etc. Especially, the parallel processes of growing a business and handling domesticity certainly made their upbringing more versatile.

My business was a decade old by then. Jain Brothers, founded on fairness and integrity, had earned a spotless reputation as a 'one-stop shop' for all agricultural and related inputs. The sub-agency of Standard Cars and an additional petrol pump at Bhusaval proved to be our most rewarding ventures. We were growing fast but the growth was happening sustainably. We then started our transport business on a big scale. Additionally, some of the most reputed names in Indian business like Zuari Agrochemicals and National Seeds Corporation, honoured us with their prestigious agencies. Thereafter, we diversified into wholesale agencies of pharmaceuticals. We also represented the top companies in this activity. Our business, which was spreading in all four directions, had reached a turnover of 10 crore rupees (2 million US dollars as per 2012 exchange rates). However, the net profit was still in the range of a few hundred thousand rupees.

I was honoured by the then agriculture minister, KM

Patil, for the best yield of jowar in my farms at Wakod. We were arduous and enterprising. Often my intuitive powers of judgment were tested. We were gaining in respectability as much as in profits. To digest the fruits of these many successes, it required humility, simplicity in thought and lifestyle, and a larger purpose of contributing to society through business.

Our Chanda (now Mrs Chandrakala Ajitkumar Surana) had written to us from Manmad. Her pen was dipped in the precious drops that flowed from her eyes in reverent memory of Kantabai:

Bhau, Kantabai has given me enough sanskaar *that will not only last my entire life, but will also be enough to be passed on to my coming generations. They are self-generative and compounding in nature. Bai (a lady of honour or a mother) always used to tell me, 'Hearts won over by sheer love and timely help offered to a needy person, are more valuable than all the gold and riches in the world put together'. Bai has taught me how to sacrifice selflessly in the service of others. She used to say, the more the sandalwood is rubbed against a rough stone, the more the fragrance it will exude. It thus achieves greatness through self-sacrifice and leaves behind a lingering fragrance in its surroundings.*

Bai was above differentiation or discrimination. She loved equally and gave equitably. I have never ever noticed a rift develop in relationships because of her biased or preferential treatment. No less than fourteen or fifteen young girls in our family, including me, have been groomed by her. While taking care of one's own family, she stressed the importance of earning a good name in society through a meaningful contribution to it. Although, we were not biologically born to her, her affection in raising us and dedication in training us was at par with that of a mother. How young girls should earn respect and admiration from others through befitting conduct; what and how to speak; when and where to do so and with whom. To learn to listen before speaking—such finer details of good behaviour and conduct were taught to us very affectionately by Bai. Not to be negative, not to say no to everything, not to display unpleasant or unbecoming matters in public by being gossipy, not to vitiate the family atmosphere by discussing unsuitable external matters…such innumerable attributes inculcated in us by Bai, have contributed immeasurably to our character building.

Bai always used to say—don't waste your positive energies in dwelling on the shortcomings and faults of others, and don't engage in activities that would produce negative results. In every household, some friction is bound to occur sometimes. But we should refrain from grumbling and complaining about this. We should avoid creating mountains out of molehills. If ever some tussle occurs with someone in the family, we should always avoid being instantly judgmental or taking an instant decision. We should always sleep over the matter. Every new day is a fresh day and will bring in its wake a solution most of the time or create a new emergency, which will make the earlier problem insignificant. We should always pay heed to what others have to say and understand the context of their opinion before replying. Many problems are born out of unmindful and inconsiderate opinionating.

We learned from Bai, tact and deft handling of situations—before opening important topics for discussions, one should gauge the mood of the other person, and be selective and judicious in the choice of words. To talk recklessly, irrelevantly, irresponsibly or imprudently is an invitation to conflict. Bai possessed this unique quality of convincing others very amiably, without rubbing the other person up the wrong way. She herself was never very abrasive or domineering. She reserved her opinions for a very few, to whom her voice would make a difference, as if she had taken a vow of silence. She taught us through her practice and not merely through preaching, that self-control, discipline, restraint—call it what you like—but collective living is incomplete without it; may it be in joint families, offices or communities.

Bai was a person of few words, but her words were worth their weight in gold. She thought deeply before she spoke. Her speaking was meaningful and never out of context. And while she used to lecture us sometimes, she never ever opened her mouth before the elders. Bai was discipline personified!

I will never forget one of the invaluable lessons of life that Bai taught me: 'Chanda, always bear in mind that it is easy to fear darkness, but it is difficult to fearlessly cross the darkness and light a lamp which will lead the family to brighter days and ways. We are born to light the way for the families that we adopt as our own after marriage'

I also learned from Bai not to insist that others should always understand you and go with you. It was more important for a homemaker to understand others and go with them, thus promoting harmonious coexistence in a joint family. Indeed, its very survival depends on such deep understanding. On this point, she had added hastily that such behaviour did not amount to subjugation as was commonly thought, neither was it so difficult to practice, 'You are not forsaking your identity by doing this. You are maintaining the family's identity by compromising and reconciling a little bit. The edifice of any joint family stands erect on this tall sacrifice of the homemaker. The respect and adoration that she earns in return is her cherished reward. Today, there is boundless joy and contentment in our two-room apartment that effortlessly accommodates at least fifteen members. I tell you Chanda, this happiness would elude any six-bedroom bungalow which does not have 'space' for aged parents in all its spaciousness.'

For a stern and uncompromising husband on matters of duties and responsibilities, a homemaker like Kantabai who left nothing to be desired, was like a dense tree under whose cool shade our family took succour.

This Chanda, who often took me on 'guided tours' into my past through her letters, was our first foster daughter. Her kanyadaan was also performed by us. Whenever I take out her letters to read and re-read them, it unfailingly strikes me that these children, mentored affectionately by Kantabai, have not only grown in age, but have also carried forward our family's customs, traditions, culture and values with age. They are the elongated shadows of Kantabai's persona. Wherever these fine young ladies of high character and moral stature have been married, they have made us proud and brought happiness and contentment in those families by their excellent conduct.

Anita, Sunita's younger sister, is one more of our 'daughters'. She once wrote: *Bai is like my second mother! My first mother gave me birth, but my second mother taught me how to make this life worthwhile. She taught me everything from formulae for herbal home remedies to negotiating the various contours of life.*' Devbala, Sunita's elder sister, has penned a beautiful short Marathi poem in praise of Kantabai:

You personify contentment and bliss,
You are our family's joy and peace,
Everybody small or big,
We adore you with sweet songs of praise.

So, although a girl was never born to Kantabai, she nurtured many fine homemakers.

And the one who moulded so many young minds, was in turn largely moulded by my mother. My mother had tremendous admiration for her. While at Wakod, Kantabai had blended with the family of twenty to twenty-five people, taking on the challenges effortlessly. During this period, she imbibed some of my mother's outstanding attributes—commendable efficiency, infinite capacity to bear pain, an outstanding knack of maintaining relationships within and outside the family, an attitude to be ever ready to help the needy and empathize with villagers to understand their problems. All these made an indelible impression on Kantabai. Almost unknowingly, she started emulating my mother. It was for this reason that my mother adored her and said, 'If there be a daughter-in-law, she should be like Kantabai! My daughter-in-law is truly one in a million, the one who can churn butter even from water!'

This fine family tradition continued even when Kantabai became a mother-in-law. Just like my mother, Kantabai too was noted for her generosity, considerateness and kind-heartedness. She would often employ the needy from amongst our relatives. Apart from the wages, she would also ensure that they were properly fed, clothed and housed. During festivals, she would give them utensils and other useful domestic items as gifts! All the maidservants loved her and none ever left for better prospects. However, following mother's tradition, she would give employment only to those who came with proper references.

The generous and the compassionate are the Almighty's emissaries on earth. On the strength of their noble deeds, they can survive the roughest of weather. Kantabai used to gain divine satisfaction in helping others. This noble quality has been transferred to my four sons and their wives. She lived a compassionate life of truth and non-violence. She was a living testimony of hard work and honesty. She was of the firm view that whatever prestige and goodwill the present generation earns through hard work, integrity and fair play, the next generation should strive to build upon. Only then can the material and non-material assets of the family prove to be sustainable. My sons and their wives, too, tread this path with noble intentions.

The institution of a joint family ushers economic stability, but that is not all. It vindicates the time-defying truth that interdependence, and not independence, is the basis of all forms of collective living. A joint family institution lends sustainability to the entire social life. It is the instrument for transfer of values in perpetuity.

My mother was a strong and resilient woman, but her strength took on some undesirable forms at times. Although kind and tender at heart, she was uncompromising in matters of discipline and obedience. She had lived a dismal life of terrible hardships and supreme sacrifices. Her life was a proof that people's strength of character is judged based on whether they surrendered to difficult circumstances and let them prevail over them, or fought and overcame them like true heroes. It was this strong-willed character of my mother that had taught me not to retreat from my chosen path, once I had charted out my course. This lesson has lived on with me as her blessing even after mother left. I wish to proclaim that whatever little recognition that Jain Irrigation has earned in the world today, is due to mother's blessings. She is the first 'patron' of this global business that stands at a turnover of 1 billion US dollars (2012 figures) today. At the time when I wanted to start the business, I sorely needed some seed capital. My uncle by then had become the Karta (functional head) of my family after the retirement of my father. My mother told uncle that whatever money the family had, must be given to me. There was a bit of an argument between them and my mother firmly conveyed to him, 'You can take this as my last and final share of the family wealth'.

I had made it a point to periodically remind Kantabai about mother's enormous contribution in shaping my life and my business. However, the 'mother-in-law' inside my mother's personality would sometimes emerge and spoil the show! Kantabai would feel very sad and disheartened on such occasions. She had no one left to turn to for emotional support on her maternal side either. This had been the case with my mother too, so in a way they both had sailed in the same boat at one time or another.

The uncle resentfully threw the keys on the floor. The other senior uncle who was standing nearby picked them up, went inside the room where the money was kept and returned with 7,000 rupees and gave it to me. That is the beginning of my enterprise. And my mother thus became the first patron and champion of this grand enterprise that is standing here today.

Once, while leaving for a religious discourse, mother had instructed Gundhar Uncle's wife to wash her clothes. However, when she returned, she found that the clothes had not been washed. Her instructions had been ignored! This was enough to infuriate mother. She vented her anger and displeasure on the clothes by furiously beating them as she started washing them herself. Kantabai entreated mother to let her wash them, but she was no match for an enraged mother who taunted her, 'You are a highly educated madam, why would you wash my clothes, eh?'

Kantabai had washed all the clothes of the entire family right from the day she entered the household. Even so, because of someone else's negligence, she had to listen to such taunts. Not wanting to bother me about the domestic front, Kantabai did not let me get even a whiff of that incident. She quietly bore the brunt of mother's displeasure all by herself. It was only when I unexpectedly came home early one day and saw mother washing her clothes that I came to know about the whole incident. I stopped mother and reasoned it out with her. Through all this, Kantabai maintained a stoic silence. Not once did she ever talk ill of mother.

Although such instances of unreasonable behaviour by mother were rare, they hurt Kantabai immensely.

In another incident, mother had once kept aside 200 rupees

on a shelf and told Kantabai, 'This money will come in handy during an emergency. So you should also remember that it is kept here.'

After just a few days, mother needed the money, so she asked Kantabai for it. A few days earlier, the shelf had been rearranged and Kantabai could not find the money in the place where it had been kept. Kantabai naturally was worried and anxious. It was a matter of trust and not just the money at such a time.

Mother was quick to get angry. The 'monster' in the mother-in-law got another opportunity to rear its head and she roared, 'For certain, you have spent that money on home expenses.' The harsh and heartless accusation was like a dagger stabbing the tender heart of Kantabai. Nobody had ever accused her on money matters. Tears soon welled up in her eyes. She said, 'It is possible that while rearranging the utensils, you yourself may have misplaced the money. I swear I really don't know where the money has gone. It is also possible that you could have given it to someone and have now forgotten it.'

How could mother tolerate such 'answering back'? Clueless as to how to respond to this unexpected confrontation, she also started crying. It was indeed a sorry state of affairs, about which I had no clue for over two years! When I did come to know about it, it was from Bhimadada Pol, a domestic help in our home.

It made me think, the two most important women in my life avoided bringing up such a grave matter to me. Why? Because they loved and cared for me more than life itself. I was the centre of their universe. They never wanted me to get perturbed by domestic squabbles that would hinder the single-minded pursuit of my dream. For my mother, I was her master creation! While for Kantabai, I was her soulmate for creation of a new world. The predictable consequence of situations—where the male member is sandwiched between the mother and wife's possessiveness and loses his focus at work, never occurred in our family. On returning home every night, I never felt I was entering a war zone. I always felt a paradise awaited me—to comfort my weary body and mind. Both the noble ladies ensured this. Just as I was their dearest, they, too, were my most beloved. While I was the creation of my mother, Kantabai was the creator of my future, our family's future. I would never have been able to achieve whatever little I have, without the combined strengths and sacrifices of these two ladies. I bow to you mother, and salute you, my soulmate.

A short while thereafter, while cleaning the home for Deepavali, Bhimadada found the money under a vessel, and returned it to mother. Rather than rejoicing, mother broke down. Hers were tears of remorse that washed away her guilt. She went to Kantabai and sobbingly told her that the money was found. She became extremely emotional while accepting her fault, 'I curse my anger and my tongue. I was so heartless and thoughtless to have uttered such unforgivable words. Maybe I am getting old now... Oh God, please take me under your shelter.'

Mother's loving hand caressed Kantabai's head in profound blessing. As if she was saying—my dear daughter, forget what has happened, forgive me. Kantabai was moved, but could not speak a word. She too was choked with emotion. She just kept on massaging mother's legs.

Kantabai had very closely observed the two sides of mother and learned how to deal with them. She would often talk about these experiences to the young girls in the family and counsel them about how to handle such potential 'dangers' when they got married.

Kantabai had passed through countless pleasant and unpleasant situations in her life. She absorbed the core learning from each incident and then shared her rich experiences with the young ones of our joint and extended families, including her daughters-in-law. She did it with love and compassionate understanding of their modern mindsets, so there was no disparity in the transmission of our family's sanskaar from the past to the present. Like every other responsibility, she handled this one too with care and concern.

What name does one give to this affectionate bond between mothers-in-law and daughters-in-law in our family? It is more like a mother's deep, silent and unquestioned love for her daughter. The smooth functioning of this relationship has proved crucial to the sustenance of the Indian joint family for so many centuries. From a broader perspective, this understanding gives us an invaluable insight into the nitty-gritty of human relationships and their successful maintenance through the thick and thin of life. We then realize the immense contribution of Indian culture to humanity.

Such large-hearted people who could accommodate each other's strengths and weaknesses within four walls, who could begin each day with renewed spirits, who could wipe their own tears and those of others' and persuade each other to get on with life, are becoming difficult to find these days. A joint family's stability depends on its members' ability to forgive and forget petty differences promptly. Just like our family, this unity of hearts is a common feature of all harmonious joint families. Alas! Such people and such families are lost in the milieu of the all-pervading modernity.

It is not possible that everything happens as per our wishes in life. However, we become more rigid rather than flexible with growing age and insist that our wishes prevail over others. My mother was no exception to this general rule. Kantabai ensured that mother's word was not ignored. At the same time, she tried to break her obstinacy and reasoned with her that such understanding and compliance could not be expected from each family member. She did this with love and caring, as a daughter, not as a daughter-in-law.

Kantabai's tone would be solemn while talking to mother, 'All my life, I have respected your wishes. In fact, I have tried my best to accommodate everybody's wishes in the family. You have seen it all. But times change. Now it is a new age, a new generation. It is not practical to expect the same mindset from these young ones. Why do you expect that the same intimacy and togetherness that we share should continue unabated?'

Another incident that hurt Kantabai very much occurred then. In our entire married life of four decades Kantabai had complained to me only twice. The previous incident I have already narrated. It had occurred in 1962, and the one I am about to narrate occurred in 1978. No complaints from my wife for sixteen long, eventful years! A record of sorts in the 21st century!

Kantabai broke down totally while telling me the matter. She began weeping profusely. She spoke intermittently, between sobs.

My younger brother Kantilal is jovial by nature. Nothing wrong in that. But wit without restraint can create tragic consequences. Harsh, untempered words would leave Kantilal's mouth in utter disregard for the person, time, place or circumstances under which he was speaking. Just such an inappropriate, unbecoming and inopportune remark left his mouth once, like an arrow out of a bow, and grievously wounded Kantabai. She cried tears of blood. Personally, I feel that it was not Kantilal's fault, but somewhere, there was a slight deficiency in his upbringing which caused him to behave irresponsibly.

I was infuriated when Kantabai told me about the entire incident at bedtime. I had never been so angry in my life. I leapt towards the door, saying, 'I will deal with him right now.' Although Kantabai was in emotional shambles, she instantly gauged what would be the consequences, if I encountered anybody in this temper. She managed to compose herself and stopped me, 'Please, I plead with you; you will not step out of this room.' With outstretched arms, she blocked my way. Perhaps, she was reminded of her own cardinal rule that no definitive action should be taken without sleeping over it.

Seeing me slightly calmer, she continued, 'I swear by all that I hold beloved, please end the matter here and now. Just like every time in the past, I would have silently swallowed this insult too. But, somehow I could not bear it alone. I needed to speak to somebody. But it seems it was a mistake telling you about it. This is only the second time in our married life that I have caused you anguish, and I promise there will be no third time. Please forgive me. Please end the matter here itself and get over it. Also help me to get over it too. I need your strength and support at this time.'

'God forbid if something happens to Bhau one day, then other than me, who else will you have to look up to for support?. You know this, so conduct yourself properly before me.' Kantilal's words had shattered Kantabai. Unable to handle the grief alone, she had told me about it, not so much as a complaint, but more to share the burden of grief.

Every Indian lady is extremely touchy about her husband's welfare. She can tolerate everything, but not unfavourable talk or anything ominous about her husband. He is everything to her. This commitment and dedication is so high that she considers her own welfare secondary to that of her husband's. 'What if something happens to my husband'—the mere thought shook Kantabai to the core. She could not bear such talk about her husband.

In every joint family, brother-in-law and sister-in-law, father-in-law and mother-in-law, have always been prone to biases and prejudices towards their daughter in-law. History is proof; such biases have vitiated the atmosphere of joint families since the times of the *Ramayana* and *Mahabharata*. The trend continues even today to a larger or a lesser extent. However, I believed that the incident I just narrated was an accidental one and an exception. Kantilal is lion-hearted and pure at heart. It is unfortunate that he has a loose tongue. Even Kantabai shared this opinion about my brother, but somehow, his nature and circumstances had conspired to create such an unwelcome incident. This was the second and perhaps the last complaint Kantabai made to me in our entire married life.

For once, she could not hold back her emotions, but then, she immediately recognized this and stopped the situation from worsening. The night passed without any damage. There were more important and pressing matters to attend to the next day, so the matter was buried. It was out of the question that Kantabai would bring up the matter ever again. No tension or ill feeling remained between her and Kantilal either. On the contrary, relations between the sister-in-law and brother-in-law became stronger after passing this acid test. The mutual fondness between them would surface invariably during Holi. Kantabai would fondly sprinkle coloured water on him, and if this was not available, she would pour tea-water!

Kantilal often remembered Kantabai at teatime. They were the only two tea-drinkers in the household. Though, I have never seen Kantabai having tea, somehow, she always avoided having tea in front of me. I knew that she was fond of tea. Whenever we went on a vacation, I would instruct the organizers, 'Regardless of all other arrangements, make sure to arrange for Bai's tea.' She would never leave any of my desires unfulfilled at any time, so how could I miss an opportunity to tease her and 'arrange' for her tea during our holidays!

Joint families teach us our sanskaar. They also train our younger generation about good conduct towards people from diverse cultures and backgrounds who visit the family. Above all, we learn to be patient; we learn to gain by giving up.

Kantabai knew my nature inside out. More importantly, she also knew how to handle me tactfully. Many people used to ask her, 'Bai, Bhau is so temperamental that living with him must be like walking on burning embers. Surely tiffs and squabbles must be a regular feature of your domestic life.' She would then reply forthrightly, 'Tiffs would occur if I did what he did not like. It is my self-imposed code of conduct never to act in a manner that he does not like. I could judge very early in our married life that he possessed immense potential to reach the pinnacle of success with his hard work. Hence, I vowed to myself that I would never let petty bickering mar his progress. I trust him more than 100 per cent. He is always free to do what he wants to achieve his goals. We never go against each other's wishes, so the question of friction being created between us never arose.' This noble lady thus became the catalyst in all my cherished dreams.

Anand Gupte, one of my dear friends, thus answered a question in an interview with Mr Jaikrit Rawat, who was writing our family history:

'In view of the difficulties she has faced and the sacrifices she has made for the sake of the Jain family's progress and welfare, it would be appropriate to compare Bai with Sita Mata. In this huge and socially active family that kept growing over the years, each day which passed without any major incident, was a relief for everyone. Bai had multiple roles to play and had to withstand immense stress and tension while doing so.

She endured all this. A vast family, the extraordinary growth of an ambitious husband's business, an incessant flow of business guests, as if domestic guests were not enough! And to add to this, the responsibility of four children! Kantabai handled such mammoth responsibilities as if they were child's play. She also smilingly endured the pain of long absences. Bai possessed an incredible amount of self-discipline and resilience. She steered the family safely through all the choppy times with extraordinary sacrifices and selfless devotion. She had unshakable faith in her husband, and she loved and revered him. Her love was like an impregnable shield of protection for Bhau. No matter how much bitterness and adversity she had to face, nothing could dent Kantabai's love and faith. What if she would have wavered? Bai was totally, utterly devoted to her "God". His pains were hers as much as his pleasures were.

'On the strength of her dedication and unquestionable devotion, Bai succeeded in creating this history for Bhavarlal Jain. She was the sole catalyst of this transformation of a man into a multinational.'

Kantabai, who was groomed by my mother, knew how to change with the times. She proved this by treating her daughters-in-law as daughters. She wholeheartedly encouraged them to make constructive use of their education. The arrival of a knowledgeable, cultured and chaste lady as a daughter-in-law is akin to a lamp of enlightenment being lit in one's home. My mother, though old-fashioned, did not mind all this change happening around her—the grand-daughters-in-law were dearer to her than the daughter-in-law! She certainly had a soft corner for her grandsons and their wives.

Shobhna, my third daughter-in-law, once told me, 'The housemaid was on leave so we cleaned a few utensils for our immediate requirement and managed to run the kitchen. But

Kantabai asked us to clean all the utensils.' Dadi (my mother) intervened promptly, 'Nothing doing. I will not let my granddaughters-in-law perform a maid's task! Their tender hands will get rough.' Bai was perplexed. She replied, 'Mother, I am just implementing the lifestyle I have learned from you, and there you are, siding with the young ones. This is not fair.' But mother's wish prevailed. A temporary maid was called and 10 rupees were paid to her to clean all the utensils.

Life in joint families is full of anecdotes that lighten our hearts and brighten our lives. The ladies in the family were unhappy with the elders and in order to demonstrate their displeasure, they had decided to go hungry. But after a while, Kantabai decided to break this 'resistance movement'. She got up, prepared a dish for herself and started eating. 'Our objection is against the elders. Food is innocent. Why should we make food a scapegoat? I will eat; you all can join me if you want to.' They all did just that.

I will not make a false claim that the atmosphere in the family was always hearty and joyful. However, Kantabai's easy nature brought some humour even to those uneasy moments.

15

THAT HORRIFIC INCIDENT is deeply etched in my mind—my slapping of young Ajit, and what followed thereafter! Whenever it resurfaces from the deep crevices of my memory, I am overwhelmed with anguish. There is only one positive side to it—the remarkable intuitiveness and presence of mind with which Kantabai handled the situation at that time. Such incidents leave an indelible impression on one's mind. Even at seventy-five, this Dada (grandfather) sometimes does get annoyed with the noisy behaviour of his grandchildren at home. No matter how much one loves them, momentarily one is irritated. However, I try my best not to let my anger get out of control. No sooner do I raise my hand at anyone, the horrific incident that had happened with Ajit replays itself in my mind like an unpleasant scene from a film, and I stop myself immediately. No doubt, we elders are duty-bound to teach the young ones good conduct, but this incident has taught me, the elder—the same! This humbling thought calms me whenever I am enraged. I am reminded that these hands are meant to lift someone up, not to strike someone. Even in the past, if I have ever raised my hand at anybody, it was like a gentle rebuke. Kantabai, on the other hand, has rarely ever raised her hand at anyone. Self-restraint is Kantabai's invaluable gift to all of us. It has become a family tradition.

The second floor of Ramesh Sadan—height approximately 35 feet. A concrete street below the house. Ajit fell from that height and hit the street! All those who saw him coming down, thought that he would not survive the fall. A cyclist who was passing by saw Ajit falling down, just like a stunt in a film. He jumped off his cycle and stretched out in a desperate effort to catch Ajit mid-air. Young Ashok was present there, but was totally engrossed in playing marbles with his friends.

Ajit lost consciousness and went limp as soon as he hit the street. It was a miracle that he survived—'The Saviour's ways are unfathomable, nobody can harm those who are under His protection.' After falling from the balcony, Ajit first hit some telephone wires midway before landing on the street. Hence, the impact of the fall was greatly reduced. Had he fallen directly on to the street, the fall would have taken his life instantly, but now the injury was reduced to a few fractures. Even the way he fell made a difference. He fell in a fetal position with his legs tucked into his tummy and his face down. Had he fallen on his back, the injury to the head would certainly have been fatal. The cyclist and some other passers-by lifted Ajit gently and just as they were climbing up the steps to bring him home, Kantabai rushed down. The mother's tender heart broke down. 'Ajit is gone,' she thought. Devastated, she took the child in her arms and sat down on the first landing of the staircase. But then, she realized that his pulse was still beating. She got up and made a mad dash for Dr Murlidhar Rane's hospital nearby. Distraught and barefoot, desperate to save her child! First aid was started immediately. By then, I had reached the hospital too. Within just ten minutes, the entire family arrived there. A worried gathering of around 100–150 stood on tenterhooks awaiting Ajit's fate.

Everybody knows how hot Jalgaon's summers are, reaching as high as 47 degrees Celsius! But a naughty Ajit had ignored the instruction of not playing outside in the heat. He was outstanding in both studies and games. His elder brother Ashok had not allowed him to play with his group of friends on the ground. A disappointed Ajit went upstairs. But his mind was on the game. He was watching Ashok and his friends play marbles from the second-floor balcony. Intent on knowing the outcome of the game, he leaned further and further till he lost his balance. Ajit had the habit of sucking his thumb and even when he fell, his thumb was still in his mouth.

My heart was full of regret and remorse. While I was leaving home after lunch, I had seen Ajit playing in the blazing heat and had slapped him, saying, 'Why are you playing in this heat?' He was so taken aback by this sudden outburst from me that he had run home crying.

Was my scolding responsible for the accident? The child would have been shaken badly by my beating and would have been deeply perturbed. Was this the actual reason why he lost his balance? I could not conceal my disturbed state of mind. Kantabai read the agony on my face. She was quick to console me, 'Don't fret over it. It happened almost half-an-hour after you had left home. You are not responsible for it.' Her soothing words relieved my guilt.

Ajit had regained consciousness by then. I pondered: Why does it always fall upon the homemakers to handle their husbands and children during countless difficult situations? I realized how tricky and demanding this task was, when I reflected upon the skillful way in which Kantabai lightened my heart with the above words. She herself would have felt the pain and agony that I was going through at that moment! It requires a higher connection of hearts to be able to understand their soulmates so well—not everybody can possibly measure up to Kantabai.

Ajit used to be his mother's shadow during his childhood. He enjoyed playing the role of 'young reporter' to her. He would tell Kantabai about every mischief his elder brothers, Ashok and

Anil, had been up to. Upon thus being 'exposed' by Ajit, Ashok and Anil would deal with him 'appropriately' later. Ajit would then retreat to the balcony and await his mother. He would break into full-throated crying as soon as he saw her coming home. Such memories often take me back to the household in the lanes and bylanes of the past.

Instilling sanskaar in children or raising them virtuously is like a purification and refinement process which raises the worth and value of the 'raw material'. To use industrial jargon, it 'raises the bar' of the 'end-product'. Sanskaar also acts as a transformational agent that gives a new, higher identity and purpose to the person being 'processed'.

No purification is achieved without endless struggle, sacrifice, perseverance, stress and strain. Even an ordinary grain of rice achieves piousness and becomes akshata (rice duly energized with the chanting of hymns) so that it can be used for auspicious rituals, only after it is subjected to this treatment. A lota, an ordinary metal container, gets transformed into a kalash (a Hindu symbol of much religious significance) and sits proudly atop the temple shikhar (tower) only after being purified through a ritual. Butter is obtained from cream only after it undergoes much churning. A rough gem becomes a precious jewel only after undergoing the agony of cutting and polishing. All these arduous transformation processes offer value-addition to the base objects, because of which they achieve an exalted purpose and stature.

The imbibing of sanskaar in family members is like transforming rough gemstones into exquisite jewels. It is essentially the process of character building. It is applicable to all humanity and can even extend to the entire animal kingdom. Sworn enemies like snakes and mongooses are known to have become full of amity in the presence of Bhagwan Mahaveer (the sage who attained the ultimate state of Enlightenment in the Jain religion). Predators and prey like lions and deer have sat amicably together before great Indian rishis. Why so? Because the higher influence, the sanskaar, has compelled them to attain nobility.

Ashok, Anil, Ajit and Atul—my four sons, today shoulder all major responsibilities at Jain Irrigation. They were not entrusted with these responsibilities overnight. They first underwent regular training, gained the necessary insight into their future roles, and after a lot of rigorous grooming, were finally ready for their higher responsibilities. In a way, their lessons in responsibility were a part of their sanskaar, which began from their childhood. Kantabai lovingly infused in them the qualities of hard work, discipline and sincerity of purpose. Today, my four sons are the four pillars on which both the family and the business stand unshakable. Without proper sanskaar, they may have been drawn into the vortex of comfort-loving, luxury-prone, aimless lives that so many sons of wealthy fathers live.

I am immensely proud of the fact that Kantabai sculpted the strong, responsible personalities of our sons, in spite of her extremely hectic and stressful life. Her day usually stretched from five in the morning till midnight, without a break. She knew well that I was working equally hard, so it was a sort of a healthy competition between us! I must concede she emerged the winner—not merely because of the hours she put in, but more because she handled multiple pivotal responsibilities, that of a wife, a mother, a homemaker, and many more.

Our home was always full of young boys and girls. Our four sons and the 'adopted' daughters were frequently joined by my uncles' children. Kantabai took care of them all. From clothes and books to fees and uniforms. Even to preparing them for their exams and contests. She was always there for all their needs. Not only that, she already had the roles of the executive chef and hostess which she handled efficiently. All this besides looking after the endless stream of relatives, business guests and visiting Jain saints. She was at the forefront in maintaining relationships and attending all social events. Due to my busy schedule, I would often not be able to participate in these events, but Kantabai managed the show efficiently.

No matter how prominent or busy an individual may become, he can never outgrow society. He has to abide by its norms. It does not grant him any special provisions to abstain from important events due to his busy schedule. If he ignores his social responsibilities, society 'punishes' him at an appropriate time. It has not spared even the leading lights in this matter. Knowing this well, I insisted that Kantabai remain present at all important social occasions, despite her hands being full with domestic responsibilities. Yet, Kantabai uncomplainingly and wholeheartedly wore this cap too. Usually, I would be out of Jalgaon for around twenty days in a month. Kantabai jokingly called me 'the Non-Resident Resident of Jalgaon!'

Children's mischief and pranks are a source of fun, as also of concern. However, I remained largely unaware of my children's behaviour; taking care of them was Kantabai's forte. This was a part of an unwritten understanding between 'Her' and 'Me', as far as distribution of responsibilities was concerned.

While grooming the children, the moral, cultural, ethical, spiritual and worldly uprightness of the mentor is put to test too. If she or he falters in this critical task, it can prove to be catastrophic. This process or culturing can happen effortlessly in the case of alert and vigilant parents. However, for those parents who neglect this, there can be trouble.

Ashok was well-built and domineering right from his childhood. He would always remain surrounded by many friends and would invariably bully them. He was very mischievous and naughty. He was also a skilled sportsman—to excel and win in all types of native games and cricket was easy for him. He was interested in everything—except studies! He would drive everybody insane with his dangerous pranks. Once, when he was just nine, he had set ablaze a Samsonite suitcase full of expensive saris that were reduced to ashes! Obviously, I would lose my temper over such disastrous pranks.

My uncle Dalubhau pampered Ashok a lot; perhaps to an unreasonable and unadvisable extent. He would give in to any and every demand that Ashok made. Such excessive indulgence is not good for any child. Kantabai was obviously worried that it would have negative consequences on Ashok's behaviour and would spoil him. But considering Dalubhau's respectable and even formidable stature in the family, Kantabai had refrained from saying a word against him. As a result, Ashok's behaviour became more and more reckless day by day. In contrast, he would also display exceptional maturity and understanding at times. He would wholeheartedly volunteer to help his busy mother in many ways. He would bring flour from the mill, accompany his mother on shopping trips, fetch water from the ground floor, and look after his younger siblings while Kantabai was busy playing host to the endless stream of guests. However, while playing 'big-brother', he would also indulge in dangerous games which could have been life-threatening.

Ashok had acquired a new craze for playing a game he called, 'Shock-Shock'. He once literally 'shocked' Anil with a live wire! The prank would have proved fatal for Anil. Luckily, he was sitting on a wooden bed. What if he were on the floor! To forcibly put someone's fingers between a cycle chain, or drop heavy objects on another's foot, were some of Ashok's frequent mischievous activities. At her wit's end, Kantabai would spank

Ashok, but also correct him lovingly later.

Ashok's debts at the paan shop adjoining our home had become substantial. The shop owner came home to collect his dues. Kantabai quietly paid him and sent him away. But later, she took Ashok to task. She locked him up in the toilet for three or four hours.

Ashok's voice was naturally authoritative and thick. Once, Kantabai overheard him bullying Gundhar Mamaji (one of our maternal uncles) on the phone, demanding some cash. Kantabai scolded him severely.

Usually, Kantabai used to handle such domestic matters on her own. She never complained to me about any of our sons, except cautioning me about Ashok's continuous improper conduct. She said, 'It is necessary to pay adequate attention to Ashok. He is growing up fast. He can stray if he remains unchecked. Your timely intervention is very essential.'

An otherwise uncomplaining Kantabai's caution about Ashok was in a way a 'summary' of our eldest child's fifteen years of a carefree life. I immediately took matters in hand. I took stock of Ashok's conduct and behaviour. I inquired about his friends. After that, I 'fixed' the problem. Since then, Ashok was never found wanting in any way. Thus, he was saved from being labelled a 'spoilt brat from a rich family' because of Kantabai inculcating him with sanskaar, our family's inherent value system, and my timely intervention.

Sanskaar and hereditary nobility of the family play equally important roles in a child's upbringing. However, the macro environment—the child's friends, relatives, and even neighbours can influence his formative years. These forces can even nullify the impact of the family sanskaar and blood-values. As parents and mentors, if we had not been vigilant about these powerful external influences, we may have had to repent. After all, cultured living denotes the middle path between material extravagance and extreme austerity.

Anil was quiet and serious from his early years. He was more studious than his siblings. He was physically weak and prone to allergies, so had dietary restrictions. Whenever Kantabai prepared special dishes as demanded by the other children, Anil had to refrain from enjoying these delicacies. This saddened Kantabai and she would open her heart out to sympathetic friends about this. A loving mother's tears at such times are as pure as the Ganges.

Who was Kantabai's dearest child? Atul, of course! For him, she did not hesitate to approach even the schoolteacher who had beaten him so badly that his cheeks had got all swollen.

The teacher gently tried to pacify her, 'I was very agitated with the students' indiscipline and rowdy behaviour. I lost my cool. I mistakenly thought that Atul was the source of the trouble and thrashed him.'

Kantabai replied, 'You beat him on the basis of a presumption! His cheeks have swollen. What if he had been hurt in the eyes?'

Just then, another teacher, Mr Dikshit, who knew our family well, was passing by. He knew that unless the matter was serious, Kantabai would not have come to the school. Kantabai told him her complaint. Come evening, and the teacher who had beaten Atul was at our doorstep.

His voice was many decibels lower now, 'Sister, you complained to Mr Dikshit. I have had a discreet word with him. Please don't approach any higher authorities on this matter. If you complain to the principal or the management, then investigations will be carried out and my job will be in jeopardy.'

Kantabai explained to him calmly, 'Masterji, please understand my motive in coming to the school in its proper context. You are a teacher who is given the highest place of respect in Indian culture. A teacher has to deal with many types of students. Self-restraint is of utmost importance for him. A teacher is his students' role model. You should be very conscious of the fact that you don't generate any negativity in the children's minds and your image remains untarnished before them. You are engaged in a very noble occupation. Please don't worry; I will bury this incident right now, but please treat the children in an objective and unbiased manner in future.' Kantabai spoke her mind to the teacher, but only after ensuring that the children were not around. She was well aware that to correct a teacher in front of his pupils could breed contempt in their minds for him.

Kantabai's literary tastes were of the highest order. She was fond of watching good films and dramas. Solving crossword puzzles was a part of her daily routine. As her domestic responsibilities were relaxed and she got more time for herself, she took to the reading of good books. Even today, there are about five-six hundred choicest books in our library at home—all bought and preserved by Kantabai. They are like a bouquet of many beautiful flowers of different colours, hues and scents! Epics, novels, compilations of short stories and poetry find a pride of place in this collection. Kantabai made excellent use of her spare time getting totally engrossed in her world of books!

We have always been emotionally attached to Wakod. We started an experiment of nightshift for workers at our Wakod farm. We even got an award for excellent yield of jwala (green pepper) in the All-India Green Pepper Harvest Competition. Our photos were splashed in the newspapers! Our hearts swelled with pride, seeing Wakod in the limelight. Any occasion to visit Wakod spread cheer in the family instantly. Kantabai would never miss an opportunity to visit Wakod, especially during festivals. Wakod had cast a lifelong spell on her.

Kantabai would take the children of my paternal cousin

Girdharilal with her sometimes when she went to Wakod. Girdhari's wife, our sister-in-law Prabhavatibai, would also accompany them. Every visit to Wakod and Palaskheda, the native village of Namdev Mahanor, was a pleasure trip. Kantabai would become the team leader of the children and uninhibitedly participate in their games as she taught them new ones. The atmosphere would be filled with joy and cheer, and innocent teasing and legpulling would add to the gaiety. Kantabai would also mix informal and experiential learning with pleasure—she would tell the children stories from the books she read, especially stories with morals from mythological and historical classics. She knew how to mix with children, to be of their age. Although, she would be conscious about maintaining an elder's respect and discipline, this aspect never reduced her enthusiasm.

To be in the midst of nature at Wakod and to spend time with the local residents were the cherished moments of the Jain family. Wakod had kept our family united and happy, not just joint. It strengthened the family bonds and enriched it with the potion of heartfelt togetherness. This is what I call sanskaar! As life progressed, my business grew. But I did not outgrow my attachment for Wakod. It did not detach me from my birthplace. In fact, Wakod and its simple, marginal farming community became my inspiration to work tirelessly for the farm, farmer and farming. I've always viewed the Indian farmer, whether big or small, rich or poor, with equal respect. This has only grown with time—thanks to Wakod!

Usually, ladies never tire of praising their parental homes and engaging in unnecessary emotional talk about it. They also like talking exaggeratedly about their in-laws, especially their husbands and their friends. It is an inseparable part of feminine nature to gossip and indulge in vain talk about material affluence, about bungalows, cars, jewellery and gems, furniture and gadgets! However, Kantabai was least interested in wasting her time on such pointless chatter. She was certainly not the 'kitty-party' type. But she did attend the monthly meetings of a ladies club that had a purposeful social agenda.

That Kantabai used her words judiciously is evident from the fact that in our entire matrimonial life of forty-five years, we would not have conversed for more than forty-five hours! Not so, even if every minute and every second of our conversations are entered in the ledger of an expert record-keeper! Once, I asked Kantabai clearly, 'My God, I realize that you have never asked for anything from me!'

'Where is the need to ask, if one gets everything without asking?' Her prompt and crisp reply made me ponder—have I ever cared to ask her whether she liked what I was doing? Whether I was considerate enough to incorporate her likings with mine and make them our likings?

Indeed, I feel so blessed to have received such superior physical, intellectual and emotional companionship from Kantabai that I hoped, her experiences with me would also have been as satisfying.

But why this 'probability factor' in my thoughts! Why not absolute certainty? Have I ever seen her dissatisfied or discontented in any way? No, there is no reason for me to even begin to think that her experiences at physical, intellectual or emotional level would even 'probably' be different from mine!

This momentary uncertainty in my thoughts was perhaps the result of the age-related physical and mental changes that had occurred in her and in me. But instead of being regretful about these inevitable and irreversible changes, why not consider them as Agni Sanskaar. It is the Hindu cremation rite that is based on the thought that by submitting the dead body to the flames, all the unsatisfied and unrealized desires also get reduced to ashes, thus freeing the soul of all remnants of worldly aspirations. It is indeed true that only after the cremation of our first marriage of bodily desires that the second marriage of our souls takes place.

When I relive that transitory phase of our lives where we migrated from being a couple to being soulmates, an altogether new meaning of Agni Sanskaar takes shape in my mind. Almost all Hindu rituals or occasions—whether auspicious or inauspicious, joyous or tragic, are solemnized in front of agni. Hence, the term Agni Sanskaar should be applied more holistically and not only to the commonly accepted Hindu cremation rite! Fire in Hindu thought symbolizes a divine energy that can engulf the malevolent or lower elements and purify the relationship that is being solemnized in front of it, thus making it sacred.

With this new perspective, I am not for a moment hesitant to accept; neither do I have an iota of doubt that with the Agni Sanskaar or cremation of our lower marriage, the Agni Sanskaar or the solemnization of our higher union of souls took place. This is how we could achieve the 'absolute' state of sublime companionship through our second marriage. I would go even further and dare to say that we achieved immortality as a couple only after the Agni Sanskaar (cremation) of Kantabai's bodily form. Today, although I exist in flesh and blood and she does not, I constantly feel we are one and we always will be so.

My children often remember how their mother fostered discipline in their lives. Today, they are nurturing the same values in their own children, taking a leaf or two from the innumerable instances in Kantabai's disciplined life. Anil once told me about an incident. Kantabai was very careful and thrifty about the children's clothes till they were in Standard X. My mother had sown the seeds of judicious living in all of us, whose sweet fruits we are relishing today. 'Learn to live with less' was mother's motto. Kantabai had integrated this principle into her life very well. She would often 'recycle' Ashok's pants and convert them into shorts. She always insisted that children wear such half-pants up to Standard VIII. Likewise, she would exchange the old and worn-out saris and other clothes for useful utensils. She enjoyed cooking everybody's favourite dishes, but hated wasting food. She did not allow the children to be finicky, 'I don't like this vegetable', or 'This is not my favourite food' were hardly ever heard in our home. If ever they showed such fussiness, I would be informed. I had a unique solution—I would mash up all the food cooked for that meal and then ask the children to eat it! This way they did not get to taste the vegetable they did not like. It falls upon the mentor to sometimes be tough in order to teach children the value of every single morsel of food. Even today, as a grandfather, I resort to this 'remedy' whenever my grandchildren are fussy about food. Our household has never had to witness the scene commonly seen in other families where mothers run after their children throughout the house with plates of foods, literally pushing mouthfuls down the fussy child's throat. The credit for this goes entirely to my daughters-in-law. It was my mother who had ingrained these good habits in me and in Kantabai. She used to tell us, 'Never be brash or arrogant in your conduct. Never break the oaths you have taken in your life. Never think lowly of yourself; always think that you are rich even if you are not. Reconcile to the realities of life. Try to imagine that you are sitting under the cool shade of a lush mango tree even if you are sitting under a lowly imli (tamarind) tree. (A mango tree is known for its sweet luscious fruit, imli is known for its sour offerings.) Such positive thinking will automatically put you in a better shape of mind. Respect and serve the elders with all your heart. Win the world with love and compassion. Learn the importance of hard physical work. It never wears out the body; it rejuvenates it.'

This is how sanskaar becomes self-generative in a family. Good sanskaar influences you from within. They represent the emotions that are formed over years and handed over to you from generation to generation. As such, sanskaar moulds and represents your character. Originality of thoughts and the resultant actions, spirituality, belief and faith systems, discipline and practices, they all have their role in the formation of a person's mindset and identity. Sanskaar has an abiding effect on your personality.

Our family tradition of continuous hard work was perhaps hereditary. In 1962, we were two families of eight to nine members living in a two-room apartment in Bhate Building. My small business of a kerosene agency was also being conducted from the same place. Later, we became three families with twelve members, plus the 'transient' traffic of guests! Around 1966, my brother Kantilal and I were staying at Pragatik Bhavan. We were two families then and the members were ten. Meanwhile, Dalubhau settled down in Jalgaon from Mumbai. So for a while, we were three families of fifteen members. As our joint family expanded, we were compelled to branch out to different places, albeit reluctantly.

By then, we were twelve members in just two families—Kantilal's and mine. That is why we moved to the apartment on the second floor of Ramesh Sadan. In the next decade, this number increased to twenty members living in four rooms. We never felt any difficulty with the lack of 'space' because the joy of living together was far more than the slight inconveniences.

We would eat from a single plate from sheer lack of space at that time. The immense pleasure we got from those meals is at least ten times more than what we get from dining out of individual plates on a dining table today. Joy does not emanate from objects and physical spaces; it oozes from the love filled in the hearts of people. This is what we have learned from our experiences. We are constantly striving to nurture these virtues in the third generation of our independent yet joint family. We spend at least a few hours together every day. If, at times, this is not possible due to circumstances, I am sad and yearn for the bygone days. Although the love between us is intact and undiluted, it has to be shared between more people now, so the share of each one has gone down but the love has grown manifold.

Kantabai was always eager to help others and to serve the elders. Apart from her parents-in-law, she dutifully served Jadabai and Rajkunwarbai, the mother of Madanbai of Tondapur. Jadabai was my father's sister. They did not get along well. They would argue and squabble over small things. At such times, Kantabai's responsibility increased manifold. On the one hand she had to tackle the elders and their petty rows, and on the other, she had to ensure that the tense family atmosphere did not affect the children adversely.

Anil had asthma during childhood. He had to be taken to Mumbai for treatment often. Kantabai used to manage this on her own. However, just because he was asthmatic, it did not make her overprotective of Anil. Once, Ashok and Anil had outstayed their playtime and had come home late. The strict disciplinarian in Kantabai took stern action—she did not allow them inside. The children wept and pleaded for pardon, but she remained unmoved. Ultimately, my mother intervened and let them in, saying that the children would be hungry. In another incident the Ashok-Anil duo broke open a piggy bank without Kantabai's permission to buy cricket gear. Kantabai meted out severe punishment to them even at that time. According to Kantabai, it was not the intention but the act itself that was wrong. It amounted to indiscipline, which she would never tolerate.

Atul was close to his group of friends. He had once helped a needy friend who did not have textbooks, notebooks, etc for school, by giving him his whole school bag! He did not tell anyone about it at home, but Kantabai managed to get the truth out of him. She then counselled him, 'Why should you be scared of helping the needy?' At the same time, she cautioned Atul that gifts should not be distributed at will—those who do not value hardships and difficulties, also do not value easy help.

May it be our sons or our daughters, Kantabai always strived to plant and nurture good sanskaar in them. She did not hesitate to ask me to intervene if and when needed. 'She' and 'Me' brought together whatever pure, mature and cultured qualities that we had, and used them for the ideal upbringing of our children. We were always confident that our children would prove to be better than us—a prophecy which is a reality today.

Almost all the maternity procedures of our Jain family were handled by Dr Chandrikabai Desai in Jalgaon. She once told me, 'Bhau, I am running a maternity home. Often, ladies confide in me about their domestic problems. But Kantabai has never spoken ill of anybody, neither has she criticized anybody. She is truly a very straightforward person. I am yet to come across such an educated and cultured lady like her in my entire professional life.'

Anju once beat up Bodki, the daughter of our maid Radhabai, very badly. Kantabai reprimanded her severely, but later explained to her lovingly, 'Look, why do we treat the needy people respectfully, why do we give them food and advances of money? Just think about it. It is our good karma of past lives that we are accomplished and affluent in this life. It should make us responsible, not unaccountable and uncaring towards the lesser-privileged people around us. Try to understand the problems and the plight of the poor. It is all predestined as to who will be poor or who will be wealthy. We don't have any right to mistreat our lesser brethren.' Kantabai, who practiced compassion as much as she preached it, had personally gone to see Bodki in the hospital thrice when she was suffering from tuberculosis. Not only that, she had also helped Radhabai in every way until Bodki got well.

It was characteristic of Kantabai to treat everybody, whether big or small, with love and respect. May it be a mason, cook, housemaid or the driver, it had become a permanent feature of Kantabai's conduct to treat them compassionately. She never mistreated anybody, no matter how wrong the other person may be. She used to think, 'One may become wealthy by earning money, but one becomes worthy only by earning people's respect.' She never behaved like a typical sethani (wife of a wealthy man) or a sahibin (a wife of a highly placed officer), and never as if she was the wife of an industrialist. She always remained just 'Kantabai' for everybody for all the time.

We make people genuinely happy when we treat them respectfully. They start working with dedication and unquestioning loyalty. They relate work with self-respect and take pride in it. Work then becomes their religion. Kantabai knew this human psychology and understood common people's needs and aspirations. If we work with integrity and enthusiasm, we are sure to be recognized and honoured some day. That was the hope and feeling which brought out the best in them.

One such 'admirer' of Kantabai was Moreshwar, whom I had brought from Wakod twenty years ago. He says, 'Bai helped me a lot during my father's illness.' His father had become very ill-tempered due to illness and advancing age. Moreshwar was very upset by this situation. Kantabai counselled him, citing a Marwadi proverb: 'Even the abuses of the elders are like streams of ghee'. She would advise us to draw from this 'nutrition', and not to get annoyed. She taught us not to answer the elders back and to follow their advice calmly.

Kantabai also inculcated the habit of thrift in Moreshwar. She used to tell him, 'We are there to help you in your time of need. But this should not cripple you. You should not become totally dependent on us. Learn to plan your future based on present resources. Save at least 10–15 rupees from each 100 rupees that you earn.' Moreshwar did just that.

Another incident narrated by our driver Ramesh is full of valuable learning.

'Once I drove Bai to the market for some shopping. She had said that she had only a few items to purchase, so she would return in about ten minutes. Just then, I spotted Anjutai and Arunatai (my brother's daughters) passing by. They came up to me and said, "Rameshbhau, drive us home." I replied, "I have brought Bai to the market. She is about to return. Still, if you insist, I will go and ask her if I could drop you home." They said, "It's just a matter of a few minutes. You will be back before she returns."

'I checked the watch and gauged how long it will be before Bai returned. She was normally very punctual. It was time for her to return. Noting my reluctance, the young ladies walked away in a huff. I felt very bad. I thought I was up for a stiff reprimand. But I was helpless. I narrated the whole incident to Bai as soon as we reached home. I will never forget Bai's response.

'She had said, "Ramesh, you need not worry at all. You have stayed true to your duty. It is true that our own daughters had to walk home, but you tell me, does everybody own a car?

What is wrong in walking sometimes? I will handle the girls if they have felt bad."

Ramesh added, 'Bai possessed an innate sense of justice. She was a thinking person and she always thought fairly. She was our family's supreme court! It was as tough as it was easy to serve in this courthouse. One had to think carefully while replying to Bai's queries. Honesty, total transparency in dealings, innocence of thought…the entire credit for inculcating these qualities in me goes to Bai!

'Bai hated sitting idle. She always told me, "Ramesh, we have some good books in our home. Read them. Or at least, read the old newspapers. Always engage in some good activity, never sit idle." It was because of this good advice that I formed the habit of reading. Bai always dealt with us respectfully.'

Kantabai did not like matters to drag on unnecessarily. Whether it was shopping for groceries, or attending weddings and social functions—she believed in fast disposal of work and responsibilities. She was excellent at 'multitasking'. While she would be kneading dough in the kitchen, rice and dal would be cooking separately on the gas stoves, and someone would be cutting vegetables under her supervision.

I vividly remember Kantabai labouring under the strain of carrying bags full of vegetables as she climbed up the two floors of Ramesh Sadan during our humble days. Ashok, I or whoever was present upstairs, would rush down to help her. Kantabai would deal with everybody with affection and equality. However, she was very particular about accounts, may it be the mere purchasing of vegetables or the expensive shopping of saris. She would not tolerate any irregularity or oversight. She was good at mathematics; she knew the multiplication tables by heart. Hence, she handled the domestic accounts and payments easily.

One of Kantabai's many unique qualities was the deft and

expeditious handling of tasks. She would also invariably start the next task on her agenda no sooner the previous one was on the verge of getting over. She looped her work seamlessly and expertly. Although she was a bit overweight, her energy and enthusiasm would put any gym-going, 'fit' housewife to shame. She put her heart into whatever she did. She was much sought-after during marriages and functions—while melodious ceremonial songs poured out of her mouth, her hands would be busy embroidering! She knew countless local hymns and folk songs that went with the rhythm of operating the hand-mill. She had also learned many Rajasthani songs from my mother. She was a genius at interweaving her husband's name in such sweet native lyrics! She had 'patented' her ingenious talent to devise such witty ways to fondly remember her husband who was mostly away at work—out of sight but not out of mind! According to Hindu customs, ladies do not take the name of their husbands. To overcome this, she had made a sweet lyric—in which she wove the name of her husband:

Name him! Name him! What is this game.

How does it benefit you by taking Bhavarlalji's name?

Kantabai was a born manager. It was her expertise to prioritize work according to necessity, preference and importance. She always carried a plan of who is to be deployed for which task in her mind. She possessed the highest intelligence and managerial capabilities, so she was never ruffled by the multiplicity or complexity of tasks at hand.

16

I REMEMBER I was searching for an able captain to head our business. I had set my eyes on Shirish (Dalubhau's son). He possessed a charming personality and was intelligent. It was 1965–66; Shirish was about ten or eleven years old then. I had taken him with me to Belgaum for a marriage in the family of Kantabai's mother. It was his first and my second trip by air! Air travel was a big deal in those days. Considering that I was grooming him for the future captaincy of the organization, the special treatment that he was getting from me was well justified. People often said that Shirish was my favourite.

Even otherwise, it was my duty to give special consideration to Shirish in my scheme of things. My father, in spite of his abject poverty, had taken the responsibility of Shirish's father Dalubhau's education during his engineering course in Anand (Gujarat). In turn Dalubhau had looked after me while I was graduating in Mumbai, in more or less similar economic circumstances. Now, it was my turn to take the responsibility of settling Shirish. This was my dharma or moral obligation as per the dictums of the joint family system. The preferential treatment to Shirish was thus nothing unusual. However, I had no clue as to what its fallout would be on Kantabai.

It cannot be said that Kantabai was unhappy in any way due to this, but she did tell her sister Shantabai in Mumbai what was bothering her.

'I have no complaint about Shirish. He is a good and deserving young man. We are doing whatever we ought to do for him, and there is nothing wrong about it. However, while doing so, is it fair to neglect Ashok? I indirectly hinted this to him the day before yesterday. Now let us see if it has any effect.'

This was the concern of a mother worried about her son. But this worry was not due to Shirish. Kantabai was losing sleep over the possibility of Ashok getting spoilt in the wrong company. She, therefore, felt that he needed time and proper handling, also from her husband. This was obvious, since she had taken it upon herself to bring up the children properly, while handling other responsibilities of our joint family. And after all, Ashok was the apple of our eye, and Kantabai was his mother. I do not think any mother, howsoever noble, would have thought differently in her place.

The matter was potentially 'hazardous'. It could have turned into a Mahabharat, if Kantabai had blown it out of proportion by adding her own prejudices that could have annoyed everyone. A vague thought did flash through my mind—had Kantabai succumbed to jealousy, as countless other women would have done in her place? Even if that had been the case, I don't think it would have been wrong—after all, mothers' hearts are the same all over the world. But, as far as I knew, in Kantabai, I had never seen the slightest trace of jealousy, malice or other such negative traits. Kantabai's exemplary restraint and discipline once again averted a major and potential upheaval in our family.

Everything that happens in life is in some way influenced by money or material considerations, attitudes of people involved, time or the background scenario. That is why, I would like to say after deep objective thinking, that Kantabai had loved, nurtured and protected the family from evil and undesirable influences almost divinely. She was so full of compassion that she had become the metaphorical mother of the entire family. I never got the chance to speak to her at length on this subject, because, as I have mentioned earlier, the unpleasant occurrences almost never reached me. In our entire married life of forty-five years, there was an exception to this unspoken rule only a couple of times.

Anyway, Kantabai never let Shirish or anybody else get a whiff of her momentary concern after that day. This must have happened due to two reasons. Firstly, I started paying more attention to Ashok, due to which there was a rapid and perceptible change in him. 'You reap what you sow'—this is how it started showing positive effects on Ashok. Besides, Kantabai had a firm conviction about my sense of duty towards the children. My keen interest in Ashok's conduct reinforced Kantabai's conviction and she stopped worrying about him. The second reason is that she had full confidence in my apt handling of joint family matters. She, therefore, took upon herself the responsibility of looking after the family as if it was her duty to do so. That in any case was her innate nature. Out of these two reasons, either one or both turned this episode into a passing event.

'Most of us are aware of the road ahead in our lives, but only a few realize the pitfalls lying in our path. Vision and clarity of thought are required in equal measure to successfully negotiate our paths through such roadblocks. Each member in a family has individual traits and preferences, the list of which is bound to be long. It is extremely trying for the homemaker to keep everybody happy and united. Our Bai was perceptive, decisive and capable enough to perform this fine balancing act with ease and élan. The responsibilities are endless—to remember the birthdate of each and every member of the family, to care for the sick, to look after the children's education, to attend social functions, to observe all customs and traditions of the family…such and many other aspects need careful attention and deft handling. To deal with everybody lovingly and to get tasks done tactfully, to lead by example and to inspire the family members to take on new responsibilities and roles—it was only Bai who could handle all this with ease. Obviously then, vision is a prerequisite to take on such a tremendous responsibility. It is not enough to know the way or have the vision on how to travel the path. It is most important to have the willingness and grit to actually travel the path! Only then, vision becomes reality. I have tremendous admiration for Bai and Bhau for these qualities.'

These were the words of my nephew Abhay, the young blood of the organization who is today handling many core responsibilities. He is our family's moving and ever-accessible 'encyclopedia'—the one to refer to for any information or news! We lovingly call him our 'All India Radio'.

These young ones, nurtured in a joint family environment, are today the cornerstones of the company. They learnt to handle newer responsibilities and challenges as they grew. At home, they were being continuously nurtured by Kantabai, while at work, the constant upheavals and pitfalls of business, groomed them to be tough and resilient entrepreneurs. I have been continuously observing and evaluating the progress of these children very minutely. In particular, I am very critical when it comes to their performance at work.

When Kantabai entered the Chordia family of Wakod as a grihalakshmi (homemaker), the strength of this joint family was seventeen. In Kantabai's lifetime, these five family trees, their branches, their offshoots and supporting roots blossomed into a massive 107 members! Oh my god, how big had our joint, extended family become during this time! How incredible it seemed!

It would not be an exaggeration to say that our joint family had grown like the tail of Hanumanji. Our family's growth was as much qualitative as it was quantitative. We were also getting able and capable manpower for our organization from the family. This was of vital importance because our company was rapidly expanding and diversifying into many areas. Between 1963 and 1975, we had taken up agencies for as many as forty companies in fertilizers, seeds, pesticides, petroleum products, motorcycles, tractors and auto parts. The tally went up to sixty-five by 1978, with the addition of some pharmaceutical agencies.

Today, when I look back, I recall that when I had started the business in 1963, the capital outlay was 11 lakh rupees and the profit was 11,000 rupees. Then, when we entered manufacturing in 1978, the turnover went up to 11 crore rupees, with profits of 5 lakh rupees. In one and half decades, the business had grown hundred times, while the family had grown to ninety!

On the birthday of Lord Mahaveer on 23 April 1978, we started our first manufacturing venture by purchasing a sick banana powder-making unit. To turn this plant around by converting it into a Papain manufacturing unit was an almost impossible task. It was as if we hated smooth sailing! We were hungry for apparently insurmountable challenges! Countless hardships and gruelling, arduous work lay before us. We were at the crossroads of so many momentous milestones! Unimaginable growth of the family and its responsibilities, and unimaginable challenges at work. We were at a historical point in our lives. I had it in me as part of my DNA to work endlessly to pursue my goals. My entire heredity consisting of my father, three paternal uncles, cousins, my brother and I, were going to be put to the acid test, with this purchase of the banana factory and its envisaged transfer into a Papain plant! We had to give it all we had. Failing was simply not an option available to us. Our family pride was always a non-negotiable article of faith.

We were ready to contribute our individual and collective might for this 'epic' struggle. The domestic front was led by Kantabai. Patience, resilience, silent endurance, an ego-free personality and absolute sincerity in fulfilling all family and social responsibilities had always been her hallmark. Without these sterling qualities, it would have been impossible for anyone to manage such a complex family. Kantabai succeeded because she had perpetual reserves of these qualities either in their inherited or cultivated form. As for me, I had inherited honesty from my father, while large-heartedness, maturity and capacity for relentless hard work were a gift from my mother. That is why when 'She' and 'Me' became 'We', we were able to move mountains. Our love and understanding made every impossible task possible.

As I have said earlier, hardships and difficulties were always my companions. Take the case of my father—a big, joint peasant family of eleven, trapped forever in the vicious jaws of poverty and constant illnesses. Epidemics, plague, drought every few years. Merciless heat and aridity, the constant looming threat of bandits and thieves; this was the kind of wretched childhood in which he grew up. When he was just eleven, he had to drop out of the fourth standard from the only school in the village, and take on all the responsibilities of the entire joint family! I would say that even a dumb animal's plight would have been better than that of my father's. A certain amount of harshness and uncompromising insistence on strict discipline obviously got imbibed in his nature due to this hard life.

My mother's upbringing too, was equally, if not more wanting. Fate had burdened her with innumerable hardships. Her mother had passed away when she was just three years old. She was left with no one, except her father at that tender age! The mere thought that a child of her age had to take on the responsibility of an entire household sends shivers down my spine. The few utensils in the mud-house became her toys, the only torn and wretched quilt in the house became her comfort, and the stinging smoke from the wood fires was her misty wonderland. Education or schools were unheard of in her village. This child had no privileges whatsoever of a childhood from her very birth. She never experienced even a fleeting, momentary touch of love. No warm hugs, no sweet lullaby, no caring or sharing whatsoever. She was literally unaware of a world beyond her mud-house and her father until she was seven or eight years old. And soon, at the age of eleven or twelve, she was married off. She was my mother, Gaurabai.

My parents had to witness the death of eight of their infant children before my birth. They had to spend almost twelve years of indescribable agony and anguish before I, their ninth child, was born. The couple would stare longingly at other couples' children, craving for a soft one to cuddle. A few moments of delight. They endured the childless years silently, not losing hope. This is 'moving on in life', if I may borrow this contemporary phrase. My hands tremble while writing this, just imagining the pitiable plight of my parents.

My father and mother belonged to the same village in Rajasthan. What they had in common was their 'ancestral' poverty and an extremely hard life that a bleak, unproductive and arid region levied on its people. Their similarities ended there. As persons and as personalities, they were very different. While mother was quite sociable and people-friendly, father was a broken man, worn out from the domestic responsibilities and hostile social circumstances. He preferred isolation to social mingling. He was a stern man for whom life's guiding principles were strict discipline and honesty. Mother was generous and kind-hearted, which made people fond of her. She would leave a lasting impression on people wherever she went. Father, though not very generous, was also of a helpful nature.

My parents were intrinsically incompatible in many ways. With advancing age, their differences grew, which led to frequent friction. Although short-lived, their bickering and sulking had become a daily routine. Sandwiched between them, it became an awkward responsibility for Kantabai to facilitate a truce. To make her parents-in-law forget their differences and to bring a smile on their faces was yet another responsibility Kantabai took upon herself! This she fulfilled effortlessly, as she helped them iron out their differences; telling both that they were right! This approach did not work all the time, so she too sometimes failed. However, most of the time she was an expert in sorting out such domestic problems. In return, she earned their unconditional affection. To the father-in-law, she meant more than a daughter, and the mother-in-law too was no less fond of her. Sometimes mother would feign annoyance just to get Kantabai's attention! Kantabai would act deftly like an astute statesman at such times. To tell the truth, both my parents were simple persons with pure, innocent hearts.

Father was so positively biased towards Kantabai that he would refuse to take medicines from anybody other than her! The logic? Kantabai's compassionate touch increased the drugs' efficacy! And mother was growing fonder of her with each passing day. As Kantabai's weight (both literally in kilos and metaphorically in family influence) increased, mother never tired of singing her praises. She thought she would live longer because of such joys of life.

I sometimes wonder how Kantabai managed to win such genuine, all-round popularity. I then realized that she possessed all the 'key ingredients' of success. To manage domesticity with amiable consensus without forsaking family traditions and customs, to respect one and all, to be worldly-wise and to manage people accordingly—these were some of her success mantras. Additionally, she was sociable, soft-spoken, well behaved, and cheerful by nature. She never shied away from hard work. Her heart was like a vast ocean with bottomless compassion. This helped her navigate our large joint family's course with benevolent ease even through choppy waters.

Kantabai was a favourite amongst one and all, young or old. While she became the 'life-support system' of my parents, she doubled up as the children's favourite cook, teacher, et al. She even counselled them about their career paths after matriculation. For the others in the family, her mere presence became a source of enthusiasm and inspiration. Whatever the matter or the issue be the chorus would be to consult the 'Bai from Bijapur' or simply 'Badi Bai' (older, wise lady). Kantabai had become indispensible to our joint family—may it be matchmaking or marriages, clothes or jewellery, hers was the final verdict.

A joint family's affairs cannot be managed with a partisan or petty mentality about division of work. Rigid compartmentalization of responsibilities ruins its harmony. All members must be ready to shoulder varying and various responsibilities as and when the situation demands: 'The work in front of me is my work' should be the approach. Then, completion of work becomes important. Who does it becomes unimportant. The list of things-to-do should be easily interchangeable with the 'who-does-it' list. However, all such things must be written with a pencil, so that they can be erased at any time. There is then great respect for traditional values yet equally great flexibility about them!

During 'peak hours', our family resembled a continuous assembly line. While someone washed the clothes, the other would be busy hanging them on a line for drying. While someone was cooking, the other was already busy preparing the ingredients for the next dish. Kantabai had a knack for seamless and flawless performance management. She developed her own style to do this. However, I would like to emphasize that she never passed any work to others, which she herself could do or to lighten the load on herself.

I suffered my first heart attack in the midst of my nephew Shashikant's marriage preparations. I was bedridden, so Shashikant was very upset. He was adamant, 'Bhau I will not get married until you are okay, I cannot imagine my marriage in your absence.' The panic button was pressed, and out came Kantabai, the saviour of all situations. She spent two hours with Shashikant, reasoning with him, until he relented. Our home was bustling with activity and a constant two-way flow of visitors, what with the marriage preparations on the one hand and the well-wishers who came to see me, on the other. When Shashikant visited us to get our blessings after his marriage, Kantabai donned the cap of a counsellor and gave his wife her first lessons in settling down in the Jain family.

'Do not pay heed to what people say about you as the newest member. All this talk about the new bride being a good or bad omen is mere hogwash. Always keep your mind occupied in some activity or the other. This will see you through most of your teething problems. Always think positive.' Kantabai thus boosted the morale of the new bride by teaching her survival tactics and dispelling all superstitions about her entry into the family at an inopportune time.

Kantabai would inevitably leave her deep footprints on whatever she did. She involved herself wholeheartedly in the Ladies Club and rose to the position of its chairperson. If she ever came across a lady with latent talent, she would not only encourage her to explore her fullest potential, but also partner her initiative. Once, a lady wanted to conduct a constructive programme, but lacked financial resources. Kantabai arranged for all the finances, and also honoured the lady for successfully organizing a grand programme! It would have been surprising if the lady had not wept out of sheer gratitude on that occasion.

Kantabai played a key role in the management of fifty-one marriages after coming into the Chordia family. This tally included our four sons' marriages, marriages in the extended family and among friends. But more importantly, in the joint family, there were twenty-one sons and daughters who got married with her blessings. Additionally, the marriages of friends and distant relatives were also under her stewardship. To participate in such celebrations and to be one with them came to her naturally. Thus, she gifted twenty-one young, hopeful couples to the society whose social value is incalculable. The importance of working zealously towards nurturing happy marriages and happy families cannot be overemphasized. Their contribution towards building a wholesome society is immense.

Let us take the contemporary concept of SROI or Social Return on Investment. It is a performance measurement of one's social benevolent actions. Its aim is to quantify in monetary terms the positive impact of social interventions.

If calculable, Kantabai's monetized contribution to society through just one activity of facilitating twenty-one happy marriages and happy families was around 12 billion rupees (around 24 million dollars). What about the hundreds of Kantabais is infinitely self-generative.

How much was I able to give to Kantabai, and how much more she gave back—the mere thought humbles me, or should I say, cuts me down to size. I am but a pigmy before her giant contributions.

Traditional Marwadi marriages are full of unexpected or even unprecedented occurrences that throw all the planning and preparations into disarray. They are a synonym for mismanagement! This happens mainly due to the avoidable harassment and the absurd, outlandish demands that the groom's entourage makes on the bride's family at the eleventh hour. And if these are not met, all hell breaks loose. Who will get annoyed, who will get angry, and for what reason, is totally unpredictable. Who will create these hindrances, what pranks they will be up to, is anybody's guess. In fact, uncertainty is the only certain aspect of our marriages. The hapless bride's family knows that lightening may strike at any time! This is a universal feature of all marriages in our community, whether in a commoner's family or a millionaire's. That is why, the bride's side remains ready with Plan A, Plan B, Plan C, etc, etc, to meet all types of unforeseen emergencies. There are specially skilled, seasoned and resourceful people earmarked just for this task. We have a saying—a marriage is to be handled and a house is to be built, one has to only experience it!

Each and every member of the groom's entourage thinks that she or he is a duchess or a duke for the day, and lives up to the role perfectly. Discarding the many sweets and delicacies in the lavish lunch or dinner, they would demand the smelly onions! Now, how does one deal with such onion-heads? And the ladies and gents groups would invariably compete with each other to see who harasses the bride's side the most.

Such are the ways in which our marriages are conducted. But I can be one-up even when I am on the bride's side. I would invariably think of innovative strategies to delight the groom's side by dishing out some out-of-this-world delicacy thus preempting their cranky demands!

During the marriage of Dalubhau's daughter Shobha, I came

up with just such an idea. It was summer, the season of mangoes. I thought of preparing dupdi, a rare ethnic Marwadi delicacy that is almost extinct from the marriage menus nowadays. This was to be served along with a mango puree. Dupdi is a multilayered pancake. First, four flat cakes are fused together with ghee. Then, the thick, rich jumbo flat cake is baked on a pan by pouring more ghee on the sides. When fully cooked, a dupdi becomes crisp on the surface but its core remains very soft and buttery. Imagine such a rare delicacy in combination with the pulp of choicest Alphonso mangoes! I was sure that the guests would be impressed and overwhelmed with this exotic dish.

However, executing the plan posed a fundamental problem. The cooks just did not know how to make dupdis, leave aside its 'mass production'. But I had already given the order. The panic button was pressed, and who else but Kantabai would answer the call. Oh my all-weather partner, you saved the situation once again! For her, my wish was her command. Devotion, thy name is Kantabai.

When I ordered dupdis to be made, Kantabai was with Shivrajbhau's wife Tarabai and Kantibhau's wife Shakuntalabai. But it was a near-impossible task to make hundreds of dupdis in a limited time, even if all the ladies were engaged in the task. However, Kantabai took up the challenge. She willingly abandoned the merrymaking and took charge of the kitchen. She was joined by the above-mentioned experienced ladies. Looking at the mammoth challenge and the limited time, I did make a concession; the delicacy was to be made only for the groom's entourage and not for everybody. A wave of relief spread over the ladies. A festive spirit replaced the tension and anxiety. My friend Suresh Dada's wife Ratnabai too, joined in the effort. As expected, the guests enjoyed and relished this unusual, mouthwatering treat.

The entire 'cooking' lasted for around ninety minutes. Kantabai had a rash on her back, caused by the heat of the furnace that was compounded by the merciless May temperature. Even then, she kept her husband's wish. To complete the toughest task on hand, come what may, was in her nature. To find excuses or to circumvent responsibilities was simply not like Kantabai. Impossibility beats a hasty retreat when encountered by formidable foes like an iron-will and hard work.

The marriage of Sukanya, Bansibhau's daughter, was held in 1970. The venue was the school ground opposite our residence, Ramesh Sadan. It was the first marriage of the younger generation of our joint family, so I was determined to celebrate it in grand style. The 'event manager' was Kantabai, as usual. The dinner for the local invitees and the groom's side was arranged as a buffet, which was a new trend then. However, due to the heavy rush of the local invitees, adequate attention could not be paid to the groom's relatives. How could they miss this golden opportunity to find fault and taunt us? They gathered in full strength and roared in unison, 'How dare you treat us like horses, making us stand and fetch food for ourselves? We are the all-important group of the groom. We are leaving. Give the food to the horses.'

It fell upon Dalubhau to plead with them with folded hands and pacify them. It was only the first or the second time that a buffet was arranged for the groom and his circle in Jalgaon. The standing and the self-service style did not go down well with them, so they had labelled it a horse's meal! A sitting arrangement was hastily made for them and a potential catastrophe was avoided.

Even Kantabai was averse to the buffet system initially. She used to say, 'The buffet system is not meant to feed people but to starve them. The hearty feeling of eating by sitting is missing in this system.'

The local ladies filled their own plates, but then they sat down in a queue to eat! So the buffet was automatically converted into a traditional feast. Now what can one do at such times, except silently watch whatever drama unfolds before the eyes.

Even in the modern buffet dinner, I had included a couple of traditional Marwadi items—dal bati and gatte ka saag, and churma laddu. The first recipe is prepared by kneading balls out of baked wheat flour using ghee as a binding agent, then deep-frying the lumps again in ghee and cutting them into manageable pieces, and serving them dipped in a curry which has baked strips of wheat flour in it. The last recipe is again a ghee-rich item; the difference being that it is sweet, while the former is spicy. The wheat flour lumps are fried just as in dal bati, but then they are ground to make a fine grainy powder called churma. Then, ground cardamom, dry fruits, sugar, etc are added to it and round balls (laddus) are made by adding ghee as a binding agent. Both recipes make a relishing, mouthwatering feast.

Serving such traditional items that are difficult to 'handle' in a standing buffet meal did prove to be a bit tricky, but by then, I was already adept at transforming difficult trials into effortless conveniences!

My adopted daughter Anju was a bright and promising girl. Petite and pretty, smart and communicative, sharp and perceptive. To teach cooking to such an outgoing young girl proved to be a challenge for Kantabai. But she found an innovative way. Around the time that I went home for lunch, she would tell Anju, 'Look Bade Bhau will be reaching home anytime now. I will tell him that you prepared the entire lunch if you prepare just three-four chapattis.'

Kantabai used to gently reprimand Anju sometimes, 'If

you don't know how to cook, all your other qualities will be overshadowed. Don't ever give others a chance to say that your grooming and upbringing was left incomplete under Bade Bhau and Kantabai.' This would annoy Anju a lot.

Kantabai had to deal with the young ones strictly at times. Respect is not always earned with leniency. The opportunity to blend modernity and traditional Jain family values with watchful upbringing would typically come up during the marriages of our daughters. Whether it was for Anju or Aruna, the selection of clothes, colour combinations, jewellery, etc, that would enhance their grace and femininity, was often decided by Kantabai. She knew the importance of a lady's dignified presentability, and recommended her choices accordingly. Which daughter would allow her mother to interfere in her 'personal affairs' in this manner nowadays? If the generation gap is the deciding factor here, why did it not come in the way of Kantabai's grooming of her daughters? I think it is more a matter of understanding the young minds and their underlying aspirations, and tactfully and lovingly sculpting them in the family mould. If mothers can do this during their daughters' formative years, the generation gap would become a defunct concept even today.

Kantabai mixed well with the new generation because she could bridge this generation gap. She would lovingly tell them, 'It is your birthright to look beautiful and feel beautiful. But mind you, if you want to find a place in somebody's heart, understand him. Take care of all his needs. Transform his house into a home with your true and unconditional love. Make his family your own and take charge of it with a dutiful sense of responsibility. While good clothes, fine jewellery and make-up will certainly make you look beautiful, these qualities will make your life beautiful. So blend these into your personality and into your mindset.' She was the living proof that happiness can be achieved in families with inclusive consideration of everybody's interests. She tried most earnestly to inculcate these virtues in the young generation.

Kantabai was an exception to the petty possessiveness in women. Her wardrobe and her jewellery box containing her few pieces of jewellery were always available to the young girls. They remember even today her open invitation to wear anything, anytime. Such mutual fondness and unreserved togetherness was the reason why they loved and adored her as their 'big mother' rather than fearing her or feeling inhibited by her.

Kantabai was a source of inspiration not only for the young but also for everybody in the family. She said, 'When confronted with apparently insurmountable problems, trust time to remedy things. Let the night pass. Darkness precedes light; night is the harbinger of dawn. That is the law of nature. Begin each new day with renewed hope and energy. Forget the past; welcome the new day with a fresh, pure and joyous heart.'

There is a unique story about my elder adopted daughter Sunita. Dalubhau, Sureshdada Jain and I had gone to a big, reputed and widely known gold and silver merchant's home to propose a marriage alliance for her. The gentleman was also a moneylender and pawnbroker. After meeting the young boy and observing the family and its lifestyle etc, we all unanimously thought that it would be a worthy alliance. We even gave a verbal approval for the proposal. However, when we returned home, embarrassment awaited us. Kantabai and Sunita's tense and worried faces conveyed that something was seriously wrong. Before they could ask us, 'What happened?' we had to pose that question to them.

Kantabai prompted Sunita, 'Tell Bade Bhau whatever you want to. I am with you.' Sunita began, 'Bhau, I don't mind if you marry me into a poor household. It would be all right even if you marry me to a small grocery shopkeeper in some obscure village. But please, don't marry me into a moneylender's family, no matter how rich they may be.'

Both had tears in their eyes! I could gauge the gravity of the situation, and kept my cool, 'Okay, we will think further tomorrow.' For the first time in my life, I was facing the embarrassing prospect of going back on my word. Moreover, it would be an embarrassment for Dalubhau and Sureshdada as well, who had joined me in making the promise. The problem was magnified when my friend Rajabhau Mayur also sided with them the next day. He said, 'Bhau, marrying Sunita to a butcher's son would be a better idea than marrying her into the moneylender's family.'

Such a strong reaction coming from Rajabhau, who is otherwise very moderate, left us with no alternative, but to take an about turn! In my life, this was the first occasion when I had to go back on my word and say no to the proposal. In fact, it was Kantabai's idea to oppose the proposal. But she remained in the background and conveyed it through Sunita, thus achieving the objective with statesman-like silence. Not everybody possesses this innate gift of remaining silent if the situation so demands, and yet getting things done. Later, Sunita married into the Bhandari family from Dhule. Kantabai even went to the US for the delivery of Sunita's first child and stayed to take care of her for over two months.

The mere prospect of talking about Kantabai overwhelms Sunita with emotion and gratitude. By her own admission, she would not know where to begin. She would just say, 'What I am, whatever I am, and whatever I have in me, is all due to Bai.'

She narrates a light moment. Sunita said 'Once my marriage was fixed, Bhau asked me 'Sunita, whichever good recipes you know, do leave them for Kantabai to follow'. Hearing this, I looked at Bai and broke out into a hearty laugh. In fact, she was my guru, it was she who had taught me all those recipes and the compliment was actually meant for her. She could have easily claimed credit, but she just smiled back at me knowingly and remained silent. That is Bai!'

There is this interesting episode that had occurred soon after Sunita's betrothal. Her fiance had come to see her one afternoon, but she was resting in her room. Kantabai welcomed the would-be son-in-law warmly, and then went into Sunita's room, 'My child, there is a guest in the hall. I am going to the kitchen; you go out and offer water to him.' Sunita immediately got up to serve water to the guest, but on seeing the 'guest', she was pleasantly surprised. She retreated a few steps. Kantabai was standing just behind her, smiling naughtily at the couple. She is still remembered fondly by the people whose lives she delighted with such spontaneous little pranks!

Sunita also remembers another slightly different episode. It occurred around the time when I suffered my first heart attack. The doctor had strictly forbidden me to climb stairs. Sunita had come to help Kantabai during those days. One day, I suddenly became nauseous. Sunita promptly handed a bowl to me, but it was a fraction of a second too late. She immediately cleaned up the mess from the floor. Just then, Kantabai entered the room. She took Sunita aside and told her something, which Sunita told me later, 'You should have called me to clean the floor. I feel very bad that being my daughter, you had to do the cleaning.' Sunita added, 'Bai was so sensitive and conscious about her duties—she taught me through this incident how to fulfill one's duties wholeheartedly, without reservation or inhibition.'

Sunita narrated yet another incident which shows how caring and sensitive Kantabai was, 'Dadaji (my father) always used to question the practice of giving a glassful of milk to the young girls every day. According to him, it was an unadvisable habit, because one was unsure whether the girls would get milk every day after their marriage. He preferred that they be given buttermilk instead of milk. Bai would feel bad about this and she would clandestinely give us milk every day! I have seen deep emotion flooding her eyes while serving us milk. And that emotion is still alive in my mind today.

'Bai used to say, "Why think negatively that my daughters will not get milk after their marriage. They will definitely get kind and considerate in-laws." Her eyes would get moist while saying this, but she would restrict the moistness from forming into tears.'

'Bai transformed our family into a paradise where happiness and contentment always flowed freely. She never let anger or malice come near her. She solved problems with love and understanding. She never used words like bullets or missiles. Instead, she would handle all explosive situations with stoic silence or a dignified smile. This is what we have inherited from her.'

Just like Sunita, each and every member of our extended family fondly treasures the many fond memories of Kantabai. They never tire of narrating such episodes and compete with each other to give yet another story about her.

Kantabai was an all-rounder when it came to handling and managing the affairs of the family. From major events such as marriages to small family squabbles, Kantabai had to deal with all kinds of problems on a daily basis. Her education and perceptive nature helped her settle these amiably. She also had the uncanny ability to restrain her emotions when circumstances demanded. Her core was as soft as butter, but her industriousness and willpower could move mountains. Her powers of decision-making were wise and astute as she kept learning from life's experiences. With time, even her occasional strictness became her asset. Everybody knew it was well-intentioned.

This is how and why the chariot of a joint family moves ahead. A key responsible person has to be at the helm of affairs. In our family, this person was obviously Kantabai. Everybody sees the progress of the chariot, but who stops to think about the wear and tear that the axel has to suffer in order to facilitate this movement? In order to minimize its wear and tear, a lubricant has to be applied from time to time. The love and affection that the new generation in our family showered on Kantabai was the lubricant that reduced the fatigue factor in her life. The young ones' affection for Kantabai was the elixir which constantly replenished her energy.

My nephew once asked Tarabai (Sunita's real mother), 'If you were to mark Bhau's and Kantabai's 'performance' on a scale of 1 to 100, how would you do it?' Tarabai replied, 'Bhau gets 100/100 of course, and Kantabai, 99/100.' My nephew was slightly taken aback by her reply and asked, 'Why not 100/100 for Bai?' The reply that Tarabai gave should be evaluated with the consideration that it originated from the mindset of a typical male-dominated society, 'Bhau is the male karta (the sole enabler or facilitator) of the family. His word is final. Kantabai has to abide by his word. Hence the difference of one mark.'

I then ruefully realized how deeply the roots of male-dominance had penetrated the cultural and social landscape of India. No matter how capable and meritorious a woman may be, she is always one step, or should I say, one mark behind her male counterpart. The reality is that regardless of the gender, knowing one's self is seeing God within one's self. And the one who cannot look within and find out the true parameters of evaluating a person's worth, will always base her or his evaluation on external and superfluous factors. The Indian lady will have to learn to look within and realize her true capabilities. Only then will her dependence on males and the resultant imbalanced and biased societal perceptions be challenged.

Who is responsible for this mentality of servitude? Is it the Indian man or the Indian woman herself? There are no easy answers. Much introspection is required. However, taking the discussion to another level, it is my belief that both men and women have got their unique and exclusive roles and responsibilities. I have repeatedly said in earlier passages that women are inherently superior to men in many respects. God has willed them to be so. Likewise, for men. These roles and responsibilities are not interchangeable. A man is a man with similar basic traits wherever he is on earth. And a woman is a woman. When the Creator has made His creations with certain predefined roles and responsibilities in His mind, then why should we petty mortals engage in futile exercises such as comparing them with common evaluation parameters? We, however, never tire of such mischievous comparisons.

My final position on this discussion is that let there be mass movements for Women's Empowerment and not Women's Liberation. What liberation, and from whom? Can women exist without men, or vice versa? Their coexistence is most fundamentally interdependent. I would go further and say that both exist not only because of each other, but more so for each other. Each is incomplete without the other. In my view, it shows the shallowness of the debater who bases her or his debate on mundane themes like competition, freedom and independence. The sanctity of this most sacred relationship is reduced due to such partisan and or superfluous views. I do not see any point in such debates.

Let us empower women, instead of liberating them. Let us know and encourage her talents. Let us employ her potential and capabilities for her own betterment, as well as for the advancement of all humanity. Empowerment will lead to self-reliance and dignity. Liberation will ultimately lead to alienation. Interdependence will create a homogenous, mutually respectful world. Independence will lead to segmentation, uprooting and separation.

A man and woman have to walk hand-in-hand, not with fists clenched at each other.

A female in any species is the only force on the earth after nature that is capable of giving birth. But she needs a man's seed to evolve and nurture life. Now, how would the activists liberate (read separate) one from the other without inviting extinction? It is in this context that I am saying that liberation in this sense will cause destruction.

I do concede that the women of rural India face a life much worse than their urban counterparts. Their plight is pathetic, and that is why it is a matter of grave concern and requires utmost attention. It is their dismal fate to face a temperamental husband and bear his mental and physical abuse, apart from bearing the entire burden of the household and, of course, raising the children. And God forbid, if it is a rural joint family, then her share of the workload and woes are multiplied many times over. The situation has remained unchanged since thousands of years for these women.

It is now more than sixty-five years since India got freedom. But the light of freedom has never reached their hearts and homes. Their lives remain largely unchanged; not any better than the mute load-bearing cattle. Even today, there are innumerable women who eke out a subhuman existence in dismal poverty which is compounded by illiteracy and constant hardship. Each day is an unbearable curse for them. This dismal reality of India can only be termed as a dark blot that eclipses its rich cultural heritage.

17

KOWLOON, HONG KONG, was mesmerizing. Countless modern vehicles flashed past us in a split second. A sea of humanity rushed about in every direction. Everyone seemed to be in a mad frenzy to overtake everyone else. Each one carried an air of immortality around her or him, and each one seemed to be carrying a lofty ambition of conquering the world in his mind. We were walking in the pedestrian lane of a shimmering tarred road that dissected the sea. We were gaping at the majestic, brilliantly-lit (even during the day) superstructures of malls and other vast retail spaces in jaw-dropping awe. Just then, Kantabai stumbled and fell down.

'Did you hit something or did your legs buckle in?'

'No.'

'Did one foot get entangled with the other?'

The same reply again, 'No.'

'Did you feel dizzy or giddy?' asked Dr Choudhary.

'No,' again was her answer.

I was left aghast. Kantabai had put on a lot of weight after Atul's birth. So I thought that her heavy-footed, slightly dragging stride could have caused her leg to get entwined in her sari and she may have lost her balance. My friend in Hong Kong, Sampatlal Dugad, Dr Subhash Choudhary and his wife Sharda (our close family friends from Jalgaon), and I were still shaken. Kantabai somehow regained her composure as we helped her up. We thought that nagging Kantabai on this matter would embarrass her and so we dropped the subject.

This incident of 1990 is still intact in my memory as if it had occurred a few days ago. I resolved to treat Kantabai's obesity at the Naturopathy Centre Urulikanchan near Pune, and did just that after returning from our Hong Kong sojourn. However, destiny had other plans in store for us.

Kantabai has always given selflessly, unconditionally. Whenever we came close, she always gave herself wholeheartedly. Even when our eyes met, there was never expectancy in her gaze, only inquiry as to what I wanted.

I went hurriedly for a bath one morning and undressed, but found that there was no towel on the rack.

I screamed, 'What is this?'

She came running from the kitchen, 'What happened?'

'What happened, my foot! I am standing here stark naked and there is no towel,' was my angry reply.

Kantabai handled the situation with typical wit and tact, 'Respected Sir, that is what differentiates a five-star hotel from a home. In a hotel, everything is in its place and can be found whenever needed, except of course the wife! I had put the towel here just a few minutes ago, but I guess Ashok must have used it and put it somewhere before rushing off to school. Wait, I will fetch you another towel.' She got one for me and left.

This was the not the first time I was experiencing Kantabai's sharp intellect and sharper wit. Pleasant expressions and ready replies being given to me simultaneously! It melted my anger. My temperamental nature was checkmated by her cool and composed demeanour.

It had become almost my daily routine to bring guests for lunch without prior notice. I was quite unmindful of considerations like whether there would be enough food cooked at home or whether there would be some special sweet dish for a new or important guest. But Kantabai would be ever ready to meet any contingency smilingly. She never failed to serve us delicious hot meals that we all relished. This had become her mission, in which mother and Shakuntalabai assisted her often. If ever a vegetable or curry was in short supply while serving, she would prepare some stored sun-dried vegetable like ker sangri, a papad dish, a vadi dish or just some gram flour cooked with onions and chillies. These would be served like a new preparation. All this would be done in no time and before anybody could notice, the replacement would be ready to be served! Kantabai would handle this so deftly that nobody, and certainly not the guests at the dining table, would ever get a hint of such shortages. Since she was not the one to blow her own trumpet, for a long time, even I did not realize that she was facing such 'operational difficulties'. When I did come to know about it, I talked it over with her the same night. While she did concede that there was an occasional problem, she did not complain! She always gave without complaining or expecting anything.

Despite all these demands on her, there was never a dearth of delicious new recipes in our household. Kantabai was an expert chef. Her delicacies were a mix of her native Kannadi and Maharashtrian dishes, blended with a Rajasthani flavour! As they say, the proof of the pudding lies in the eating—so I made it a point to go home every day for lunch, closing my shop for an hour or leaving it in someone's care. By then, our economic condition was a bit better, but we were still living in a rented house. Regardless of the home being a rented one, the joy of going home for a delectable meal was such a pleasant experience. I went home for lunch without exception.

However, on most nights, due to very pressing time schedules, reaching home at unearthly hours (around midnight) had become a rule rather than an exception. Often, while going home, I would notice families returning from the night show of a film. Kantabai would be waiting for me, but even if she had dozed off from the fatigue of the day's work, she would wake up with a start on hearing my footsteps. By the time I freshened up, a plate filled with steaming vegetables and fresh hot rotis would be ready. While having dinner and even later, she always gave without demanding, she did this all her life.

And what did she give? Love. She loved the entire extended joint family, she loved our four sons, and she loved me. She loved one and all unselfishly. She spread her love on the family like the sun spreads its light without discrimination. She even loved the helping hands and the maids with equal love, not to mention the entire neighbourhood. Kantabai was like a rich, dense tree. And the extensive shade of her love and compassion had 'space' for all of us to relax and relieve our stress and strain. To use another metaphor, Kantabai was a perennial, unrestrained stream of affection. Her love sprang from her heart. She was caring and compassionate by nature. Hence, it never occurred to her to be selective when it came to sharing it. She gave freely, in abundance, to everybody. She never did anything superficially.

Kantabai loved our four sons as much as she loved me. Had this not been the case, the sons would never have loved us the way they do—love is after all intrinsically reciprocal, it flows equally in both directions. The unrestrained affection with which the grandchildren and others in the family love me, and the way in which they used to love her, can only spring from a perennial source. In this case, it was Kantabai's heart. I sometimes think, can such pure and unselfish love be self-generative? Does it flow in the cultural DNA and hence get carried on in a family tree? Or can it be multi-propagated and transferred to the coming generations as a cultivated sacrament?

Kantabai never had any regrets or felt belittled about reconciling or giving up anything. I personally think that such an absolute lack of ego can develop only in a perennially loving heart. Egos do not allow a person to bend. But Kantabai never gave me a chance to bend! She would not let me get the slightest hint, even if I had unknowingly done something that might have displeased her. She harboured an undying conviction in her heart that whatever I did, her welfare was sure to be in it. Hence, the question of her getting displeased with me never arose. I have felt this oneness of heart and soul with her not just a few times, but innumerable times. Therefore, our long physical separations never resulted in any loss of mutual affection. We never drifted away from each other. We were always one.

Our itinerary for that ten-day vacation was Thailand (Bangkok and Phuket), Singapore and Hong Kong. We were amazed when we landed in Bangkok. Its airport was called Suvarnabhumi (The Golden Land). The hotel where we stayed in was named Hotel Rama International. Before 1946, Thai royalty began their family names with the prefix 'Rama', implying the high royal stature of Lord Rama. Ayodhya (capital city of the *Ramayana* epic) finds a notable mention in the history of Thailand. It is possible that this Ayodhya may be a different city from the one we know of in India today. However, there is a distinct Indian influence on Thailand's history—one proof is the prominent traces of Sanskrit and Pali languages in the names of their people and places as well as customs and traditions. A thought passed through my mind—this land, once a part of the pan-India map, is today so vastly different from India and the Indian culture.

We had just settled down in our hotel room when there was a knock on the door. I opened it. A hotel employee was standing there. What he said gave me a shock: 'Sir, would you like to have a female body massage?' I frowned on hearing this, 'What is female massage?' Now, it was his turn to get shocked, 'Sir, it means your body is massaged by a young, good looking female masseur, and of course, if you like, you can keep her after that.' I sighed in despair, said, 'No, thank you,' and shut the door after him.

Returning to bed and lying down, I narrated the exchange to Kantabai, and then added a naughty teaser, 'So, shall we proceed for a massage?' Kantabai was more than a match for my humour, 'I have no problem if you want to attend a 'massage festival', but I am not coming. Why should I seek help elsewhere when I have a great masseur at my disposal here who can cure my aching back right now?'

Thailand, once an integral part of greater India, has today undergone a sea change. I can understand change, but such radical change that uproots one's original culture and values! The next day's newspapers made my head spin. They were full of women in various stages of undress advertising their services. They were legitimate advertisements with phone numbers, licence numbers, rates, and much more. I was stunned with disbelief. Such immoral activities going on in a hotel named after Lord Rama? Upon inquiring, I learnt that 'Body Shopping' was a major source of earning revenue for the country. Many tourists from all over the world thronged Thailand because of this singular attraction. We felt disgusted but helpless. We had no other option but to turn our face the other way. Inviting the Chaudhary couple from the adjacent room for a chat provided some relief to our shocked minds.

We flew to Phuket the next day. The chairman of Riblock, Mr Bill Menzil, and his wife Gerda had come to receive us at the airport. They welcomed us warmly. We came to know that if we paid a fixed amount, we could rent a majestic beach-facing bungalow and live there like royalty! The view from our bungalow was fantastic. The blue water was as transparent as glass. My friend Dr Chaudhary and I rented a water-scooter to ride on the sea. Kantabai and Mrs Chaudhary watched us from the shore. I took the driver's seat while Dr Chaudhary sat on the pillion. It was a Honda scooter, so I was assured of its rugged quality. I drove fast. Though the sea was deep, the water was so transparent that we could see the seabed clearly.

I was in a macho mood. Like a hero, I ventured five or six kilometres into the ocean. Dr Chaudhary was a bit rattled by this bold adventure. He lost his balance for a moment, which caused both of us to slip off from the scooter. However, we clung on firmly, and were saved from falling off. But Dr Chaudhary's glasses did fall off and landed on the seabed. By sheer luck, I did not lose mine. Now, how were we to retrieve Dr Chaudhary's spectacles? We could see them lying on the seabed but there was no way to get them back. I could not leave the driver's seat, neither could my feet touch the sea floor. As for Dr Chaudhary, how could he spot his glasses without his glasses! In the end, he somehow managed to retrieve them. Meanwhile, our respective wives were on tenterhooks on the beach. They started screaming at us, but we could not hear them. A happy ending ensued after a few minutes of high drama at 'high sea', when we returned to the beach in one piece.

The bungalow had a full-fledged kitchen. Kantabai and Mrs Chaudhary took full advantage of it and started preparing one delicious delicacy after the other. It was as if they were on a health-improvement mission for their husbands! Bill and Gerda also joined us often and enjoyed our company. Gerda even ventured into the kitchen for some cooking lessons. We left Phuket for Singapore with a heavy heart. On our way back, we made a stopover at Hong Kong.

It was a memorable vacation, particularly so because as their collaborators, we were Bill and Gerda's honoured guests. Bill Menzil is a formidable name in plastic processing. 'Riblock Pipes' is his invaluable gift to this industry. Its patent is also in his name. It was apparent from our very first meeting that we were like-minded entrepreneurs. I will always remember Bill as a fine man of refined qualities and a lion's heart. Prior to this 1990 vacation in Phuket, he had also sponsored and accompanied Kantabai and me on a wonderful voyage in and around Australia. He owns a yacht that has excellent accommodation and gourmet food, apart from recreational and other facilities. We stayed on the high seas for seven or eight days. A special feature of this voyage was that 'She and Me' were on our own for the entire vacation. No friends from Jalgaon accompanied us on this trip. For this reason, it was certainly an exceptional holiday.

We were totally relaxed and spent time chatting, playing cards, even steering the yacht! And if we got time off from merrymaking, we would discuss innovation and research in the plastic industry. It was a truly pleasurable and exhilarating experience. I had found a true friend in Bill. Kantabai, too, soon became friends with Gerda. I have always believed that good and true friendship is not purely a matter of chance. Such enduring friendships can also be cultivated by choice. Once such a friendship blossoms, it fills our hearts with indescribable joy. One has to do one's bit to sustain such friendships, but then, the spirit of mutual understanding and support comes automatically once a friendship is heartfelt. Such sweet friendships cross geographical borders and travel beyond the boundaries of faith, caste, creed, language and nationality.

There was this endless ocean extending beyond our vision, there were the twinkling galaxies looming low in the night sky, and there was my soulmate who lit up every moment of my life. All thanks to the Menzils who had gifted us these treasured and invaluable intimate moments. It was truly a memorable and fabulous vacation. Bill and Gerda visited us in Jalgaon many times afterwards. Their visits became celebrations of a cherished friendship. For them, it may be professional etiquette to treat the core business circle importantly. However, considering my rapidly growing business and equally fast-expanding extended joint family, I found it to be rewarding to adopt such practices. Hence, I have always embraced like-minded associations that enhanced the business and also nurtured heartfelt friendships. As long as 'She' was there, and even after 'She' left, I have carefully cultivated such relationships. They prove to be equally invaluable for a dynamic large business house as well as a dynamic large family. They add important dimensions of multiculturalism and a worldview, in both the work and the domestic scenarios. They even help the younger generation to understand each other and bond better.

Later on, after Ashok got married in 1986, both generations of our families went on vacations together to various places, including Nainital and Rome. 'She and Me' were of course an indispensible part of such happy holidays. The vacations in Nepal and Ooty were also highlights of congenial family enjoyment. We naturally felt like relaxing after the entry of Ashok's wife into the family. Anil, Ajit and Atul were also on the verge of completing their higher education. We were able to accrue many benefits in life because of Kantabai's nature of emphasizing domestic responsibilities and her superior management capability. The business was rapidly gaining momentum. It was a big leap into an ambitious future! Initially, profits were low in spite of a high turnover, but later, we could see some money in our hands.

Who does not like vacations and outings? But the time that we take out for such leisure should be opportune; leisure should not be enjoyed at the cost of responsibilities. Each moment of enjoyment should have the permission of time and circumstances! There were times that my travel plans would change. Sometimes, I had to leave in the middle of a lively social gathering while on a vacation, when work suddenly called, or delay joining the holiday-makers due to unforeseen and unexpected situations at work. I remember, we had planned a vacation to Mysore, Ooty and Bangalore in 1985, but I was suddenly held back because of work. So Kantabai and the families of Dr Choudhary and Dr Doshi left as planned, while I joined them a few days later. I had to abandon the Nainital vacation midway in 1987. I hear that nowadays if there is some change even in a film-going programme, people start preparing divorce papers! Oh God, we were certainly a better lot!

The Ooty vacation will undoubtedly be the best in my life. If I was asked, 'Which were your best moments of domestic bliss?' I will shoot back with absolute certainty, 'When I was sitting on a swing in Ooty and Kantabai was gently rocking it like a cradle.'

I have always given first priority to work and business, notwithstanding my fondness for enjoyable vacations. She, too, never hindered my work with absurd questions like, 'Then why did you marry?' Leave aside being a nagging wife, she never even expressed her displeasure on such occasions. She was mature enough to understand my priorities. Once, after the treatment of Kantabai and Anil was over at the Naturopathy Centre Urulikanchan, the family joined them there and we all went up to Mahabaleshwar. This was the way we fulfilled each other's expectations and nurtured each other's emotions, unconsciously and without discussion. To thus give in to the family's wishes, notwithstanding pressing business responsibilities, is a difficult call. However, I had made it a point to take breaks—short or lengthy ones with the family. At this point, I would like to express the unspoken but strong understanding that existed between us on this matter. It was not always possible to go for vacations every year. Sometimes, we knew that we would have to spend five years reminiscing about the happy memories of the last vacation. On the other hand, a vacation could materialize in the next year itself. But we did not mind the uncertainty. There was an unfailing conviction in our hearts that regardless of a vacation materializing or not, the intense desire for sharing quality time in close togetherness was present in our hearts. If we could manage a vacation, fine. If we could not, there were no regrets or complaints whatsoever. All that you need is mutual affinity and keen sensitivity towards each other. This will lead to a better understanding between couples! In 1991, Kantabai had to go to America for the delivery of our adopted daughter Sunita. Although our son-in-law was there to attend to her, I could only manage to join her for the last ten days of her stay.

Our vacations were not mere manifestations of pent-up physical desires, neither were they some kind of a compromise formula for balancing work and play. They served the higher purpose of bonding our souls. We experienced our spiritual dimension during these vacations. We cherished our love at a metaphysical level. We did not go for vacations merely because 'she' perceived them as her right, and it was my duty to provide them. The quality of time that the husband gives to his wife is more important than the quantity. The endearments that are shared make these moments golden and forever glowing. According to me, it matters more how much a couple becomes one from within, than how much they engage in frivolous fun activities. No matter where we went for vacations, we created a paradise of our own there. And no matter how beautiful the place was, it was no match for the heavenly bliss of our own universe of love. I can say with absolute conviction that at some exotic location in this universe, we scaled spiritual heights where no other loving hearts had reached before, and there, looking into each other's hearts through our eyes, we transformed from being a couple to being soulmates. When your souls are one, it is madness to count the days, hours and minutes one spends together.

Becoming soulmates was our biggest, and our only achievement in life. There can be nothing more significant than this achievement. Whatever moments we spent together, we welcomed them wholeheartedly. We were immersed in the sheer and sublime love that filled those moments. And when our vacation ended, we emerged from our own paradise and returned to earth. We felt rejuvenated. Every time, we felt as if we had discovered an unknown aspect of each other. It felt divine.

Three successive decades of my life—1962 till 1992 were full of exceptional and explosive growth and progress. Our flag was indeed flying high. I had successfully converted the sick banana-processing unit into a Papain manufacturing plant in 1978. Gradually, we earned laurels in this field. We created a record by exporting Papain of the purest quality for the first time from India. In just a decade, we put the names of Jains and Jalgaon on the world map by becoming the first and the largest Indian manufacturer and supplier of highest quality refined Papain to the world. Our rapid progress was already creating waves. We started our PVC pipe unit on Independence Day in 1980. In this field too, we became the country's largest manufacturer in just six or seven years. Receiving awards and recognition became almost a daily affair. We entered the Drip Irrigation business in

1987 in technical collaboration with James Hardy. Today, Jain Irrigation is the second largest micro-irrigation company in the world, and the largest in India.

It is not possible for anybody to succeed so dramatically without his or her share of failures. Even the mighty ocean waters are sometimes rattled by tsunami waves. During 1987–88, two cargo ships carrying our imported resin were hijacked by pirates at sea. It was a body blow. The sheer magnitude of the financial loss would have drowned us in bankruptcy, but for the timely bail out by our bankers. It was an ordeal from which it would have been impossible to come out without the courage and dedication of our company's associates. The Indosuez Bank gave us invaluable support. In a year or two, we were back on track because of our continuous hard work. Our turnover of 11 crore rupees in 1987 reached 15 crores in 1991. The profit soared from 5 lakhs to 9 crores! These feats sound incredible, but who can look beyond the success and appreciate the untold hardships and sacrifices we had made to achieve this success! We had made it a point not to let the problems at work adversely affect our domestic happiness. If one's needs are limited, then one does not have to shed tears of blood during difficult times. What is required is to be thrifty and cultivate judicious spending habits.

I still remember the old Rajasthani tradition of the wife of a soldier offering him jaggery as a token of good luck when he goes to war. Kantabai had done just this when I had ventured abroad for the first time in search of international customers for Papain, and earlier, when I went to bid for the defunct banana powder processing unit. Her solemn and resolute figure at that time, radiating silent strength, is unforgettably etched in my mind.

We entered many diverse businesses during this period. Some succeeded, some did not. It was as if our horses were running in all directions in the business field, keen to conquer new frontiers.

Innumerable agreements were signed with domestic and international companies. Many manufacturing facilities were established, some were transferred to new locations. We started a large office in Mumbai. We started manufacturing plastic sheets. We formed approximately ten to twelve companies. A pipe factory was established in Chennai. Prior to this, we went public, and brought out a rights issue soon after the maiden equity issue. Ashok, Ajit and Anil formally joined me in business from 1986. Atul would come and go as required. Later, he and my nephew, Abhay, joined the business full-time in 1991. Although all the three brothers of our joint family were engaged in independent businesses by then, the sons made up for their absence. My cousin Girdhari remained with me in business. I had made some very good friends who stood by me resolutely after the division of the family business. Prime among them were Arun Ajgaonkar, S.V. Patil, S.M. Udani, G.H. Naik, R.B. Jain, J.J. Kulkarni, Subir Bose and H.R. Handa Saab, to name a few.

After my first heart surgery in 1983, I regained in good health. I never had even minor aches and pains, neither colds nor coughs! I made thirty-one business trips to twenty countries. On an average these tours were normally of twenty days duration. Besides, quick hops to Delhi and Mumbai would occur every few days. For almost twenty to twenty-two days in a month, I was on the move, as if I had wheels on my feet. Worse, Kantabai got just a few hours prior notice before my intended foreign tours. Even I did not know when and to which place I would have to go; they were all eleventh hour decisions. I would leave for the station or the airport directly from the office, and Kantabai would send my baggage and food there. She kept an emergency bag ready for such flash tours. She tried her best to match her feet with the mad pace of life. She never harassed me with nagging questions when I was leaving on important business tours. It was just not in her nature to argue over petty issues that she considered secondary to my zeal and ambition. She was so adaptable that she made it all seem effortless. But wives of businessmen from anywhere in the world will agree with me that such adjustability is anything but effortless! Due to her uncomplaining nature, it never occurred to me to pause and ponder, 'How will she manage everything in such a short time?'

Our lives were purposefully poised for exalted, creative causes. We never thought it necessary to waste time in negative or worthless debates on the fairness of conduct. It was all dictated by circumstances, and we accepted every situation as it unfolded before us. This, in short, was our life's motto. While I roamed the world to expand my business and take it to the level of my global vision, Kantabai immersed herself wholeheartedly in her world of meaningful, peaceful domesticity. Only 'She' and 'Me' knew how difficult it was to build our separate, but combined visions in this manner. However, such a frantic life started levying a heavy toll on the body.

The evening of 26 June 1982 proved almost fatal for me. While in a meeting at the factory, I had a massive heart attack. Kantabai had then taken Atul, who had high fever, to Dr Lodha's clinic. She was already a bit tense because of this. The driver reached the clinic and told Kantabai, 'Bade Bhau has asked for his Nehru kurta-pyjama.' Kantabai was puzzled. She wondered; although it was never certain when I had to go where and for what purpose, it was always a safari suit that I asked for, never a kurta-pyjama that I normally used for sleeping in. She reached home lost in thought.

Just then, my nephew Abhay reached home (Ramesh Sadan) and told Kantabai in a breathless voice, 'Bai, you need to rush to the factory immediately.' Kantabai was taken aback. She had never been called to the workplace in this manner. To add to this, first the oddity of asking for the clothes and then the desperateness in Abhay's tone—her sharp mind could gauge that something was very wrong. She said, 'Tell me straightaway why have I been called to the factory?' Although Abhay was shaken to the core, he managed to reply in a composed tone, 'Bade Bhau is a bit unwell, please come fast.' Kantabai's mind pressed the panic button. Without wasting a second, she immediately rushed to the factory, barefooted, unconcerned about everything else but her husband's welfare. Her mind was full of ominous thoughts.

My condition was critical. The doctor had been called. Kantabai had narrated the whole situation that developed thereafter in an interaction. 'His (my) presence of mind is commendable. Considering his critical condition, he was aware that even a second's delay in treatment could prove to be fatal. Hence, in spite of being in such a life-threatening condition, he instructed them to keep a car ready on both sides of the Amalner-Surat railway level crossing which was located on the doctor's route to the factory. Such an arrangement meant that even if the level crossing was closed for vehicular traffic, the doctor when he arrived could get down from his car; walk across to the car on the other side and continue travelling, thus saving crucial minutes! With one more instruction not to move him from his position, he slipped into unconsciousness.'

I remained heavily sedated for the first forty-eight hours. Even Kantabai was not allowed to see me for the initial four to five hours. I was critical even after regaining consciousness. By then, Kantabai had regained her composure. Refreshments were already arranged for the visitors outside. The doctors had advised total seclusion and rest for some time. The wheels on my feet were detached and sent for badly needed servicing!

I rested for six months. The bypass surgery performed in the US in 1983 was successful. I prepared my will before being wheeled into the operation theatre. Only Kantabai was present in the room then. Even though she knew that I was writing my will, never once did she inquire anything at all about it! Perhaps, she thought that I was indulging in a worthless exercise—she was unshakable in her faith that nothing would happen to me, that I would emerge unscathed from the crisis. She was as calm as me. Not tears but strength of character filled her eyes. Such an inspiring attitude, even in those days when bypass surgery was new and its success was considered a rebirth of the patient. This was her strength of character!

My father passed away on 9 March 1990. He would mostly remain indoors due to his age. He had given me solid support during the initial phase of my career. I felt his loss very sorely. Although normally full of self-confidence, I was totally disoriented when father departed. I withdrew into a shell. I was constantly lost in thoughts of the past. Exactly twenty days after my father's demise, I had another heart attack on 29 March. I was in our Mumbai office then, taking an interview, when I got the attack at around 11 am. Soon after recovering from it, I started to quickly finish the incomplete tasks.

In 1991, my heart condition worsened progressively. I had to go to the US for angiography once again, but no further treatment was recommended, except some changes in the drug regimen. I immersed myself in rigorous work once again. Kantabai too felt relieved with this diagnosis.

If there was one thing Kantabai was proud of, it was her husband's personality, his character and his transparency. She often, forcefully, expressed her conviction and faith in me. One of our relatives once asked her casually,

'Bai, looking at his ambition and frantic pace of growth, Bade Bhau seems to have given an open invitation to constant stress and tension. It would have been better if he had chosen to be an advocate. He had passed the Law exam with excellent grades. Going further, he could have earned high respect from the government also. A palatial bungalow, motorcars, assistants and attendants—he could have lived a comfortable life without these tensions. Instead, what you have today is a rented house even after years of slogging. Don't you ever talk about it with Bhau?'

Kantabai's astute reply was more like an unwritten but ardently applied Mission Statement of our lives, 'If he had chosen the easy path, no doubt we could have attained the heights of comfort you mentioned. But lost in that self-centred life of our own luxury and conveniences, would we have been able to think of others' problems? Would it have been possible to hold together and sustain so many people as we are doing today? Such a vastly spread-out business and the social gains accruing out of it, would we have been able to serve people, had we chosen to live for ourselves? Our comfortable life today is the result of decades of excruciating hard work. The comforts of an advocate or judge's life and that of ours may be the same, but the lives as such are vastly different. I do concede that the tensions, the heart attacks—have affected his health very badly. But then, had he not given 'an open invitation to constant stress and tension' as you put it, would he have been able to provide livelihood to five thousand families? Can an advocate or a judge ever benefit others in this manner? We have the good will and blessings of these people, and perhaps that is why we are saved from every calamity, every crisis. Whichever path he has chosen, it is good for me, for us and for the people around us. He chose that after a great deal of thought and what he did was always right!'

After returning to Jalgaon from my bypass surgery in 1983, a thought gradually took shape in my mind, and within no time, it became forceful and persuasive. No, it was not the fear of my own death that bothered me per se. But I thought, 'God forbid, if something happens to me tomorrow, then what will be the condition of this large joint family? True, I am not indispensible. Life will go on after me. Everybody will ultimately get over my loss. But our joint family was founded on just one load-bearing pillar, and that was me. What would happen to this edifice after that pillar crumbled? Who would keep the family united in numbers and undivided at heart after me? If the family disintegrates, if family feuds reach the courts, our family name would be disgraced. Our family had an unbroken, century-old tradition of rare unity and togetherness. Our sanskaar was based on discipline, hard work, resilience and reconciliation. Would these traditions be carried forward after me? This family, which was synonymous with compassion and discipline, would it continue to be known for the same qualities after me? I could foresee a big question mark posed on the very ethos and joint existence of our family.'

So many upsetting and unsettling thoughts filled my mind.

It was time to answer all these questions. One night, it suddenly struck me that the unity of the family should be preserved at any cost—its joint-ness was beyond even theoretical discussion. However, the businesses can and should be divided. I was deliberately not discussing this idea with anybody, not even with my soulmate. The only reason why I did not discuss it with her was that the matter was related to business and not family. The division that I had in mind would divide, or should I say distribute, only the family wealth and joint businesses, not the hearts. Blood cannot be separated by any agreements or deeds; neither should blood relations be adjudged by bank balances and assets. They should be nurtured with extreme sensitivity and a deep understanding of their soft and fragile nature. Like in the case of every other subject, Kantabai did not show undue inquisitiveness about this matter of the family's separation even after it was implemented. Nor did she ever ask me about it. Why? Only the Almighty or she has an answer to it.

As I have said earlier, in the past twenty-five years, from 1961 to 1985, Kantabai had handled many family marriages with affectionate care and efficiency. Hence, we were largely relieved of this important family responsibility. All these couples were well settled in their marriages and were fulfilling their domestic responsibilities with utmost dedication. However, when it came to business, the same feeling of togetherness and unity of hearts seemed to be gradually fading away. My cousins' children were no doubt very proficient at work, but their attitude towards work was changing. They insisted that all Sundays be free days. They were not punctual in the morning and would leave the workplace at will. If they were newly married, then they would frequent their in-laws place, etc. I could observe these changes in them despite my extremely hectic life. That is why I thought that unless I imposed responsibility on them, their attitudes would not change. Their strengths and potential would only be fully realized when they were given inescapable responsibilities. If they remained lax now, it would obstruct their future growth and could even cause friction and tussles in their ongoing and future relationships.

My children had completed their education and training periods by then, and their marriages were due. All these years, I had enjoyed the final say in the marriage matters of my brothers' and cousins' children. I had a completely free hand in the planning and execution of these marriages. Now, when it came to my own children's marriages, it was possible that my conduct might be perceived as preferential in some way or the other. Elements like jealousy, comparison or malice may pollute their hearts, even if they did not voice these openly.

I wanted to avoid this possibility at any cost, no matter how remote it might appear. I wanted to be thought of as a fair and compassionate father to all of my family's children, not just my own.

In due consideration of all these factors, I thought it was necessary to split the combined businesses and let each one handle their share independently. I took the difficult decision in 1986 and called everyone home to convey it. I was very pained while I talked. All eyes were moist, including mine. It was a sad decision, but an unavoidable one. When I put the matter in its right perspective and explained the pragmatic considerations behind what I was doing, everybody agreed to it. My brother Kantilal did not attend the meeting in spite of being called to it. Everyone endorsed the decision, however, with a heavy heart.

I had prepared the minutes of this meeting. Only my friend and I knew about it, since I had dictated it and he had written it. Based on the minutes, I prepared and proposed a two to three page formal separation agreement of the joint family businesses and wealth. Everyone signed it without even reading it. Thus, I broke the family tradition, albeit for a good cause. After all, the division was to be of the family wealth and business, not of the family.

Kantabai and my parents were not aware of this division, because it would not affect their domains of day-to-day and administrative matters. Hence, it did not concern them in any way.

The family still had eighteen young members, including my four sons, who were as yet unmarried. It is remarkable that even after the said division, my parents and Kantabai continued to fulfill their duties most earnestly. All the eighteen marriages were accomplished with the same enthusiasm and togetherness as the earlier ones. It seemed as if there was no division in the family, not even of the businesses and the wealth, because the true wealth of integrity and unity was intact! This is what I call family sanskaar! Such exceptional likemindedness in such a big family could not have been achieved without the large-heartedness of my three uncles and my brother. But wasn't that a part of our sanskaar too?

In a separate document, I had declared that I would bear 50 per cent of the expenses incurred in the marriages of my uncle and nephews. What happened in due course is history. I did not have any mentionable liquid wealth. Except Shivrajbhau, all of us were still living in rented houses. We had an understanding from the very beginning that whatever we earned would be ploughed back into the business to nurture its growth and development. This was our guiding fundamental: 'Business comes first, everything else must come after'.

18

WE WERE SEATED in the grand conference hall of a magnificent hotel in London. The company's finance manager, Mr Udani, addressed the audience first, which was followed by my son Anil's speech. Then, I spoke about the company's history and forward planning for its aggressive growth plans. After the ovation, the shareholders asked many questions. One of them said, 'What you have said is okay, we do agree that the company has an excellent track record and a bright future, but where is the succession plan to handle all the future growth that you talked about?'

In short, the shareholder was asking, 'What after you?' I was about to answer him, when another shareholder stood up and said, 'Oh come on, what a question! There is this visionary father who is around fifty years of age, then there is this young, intelligent and spirited son who is around thirty, and there are also his three brothers, each with a couple of sons. Can't you see that the consolidated picture of the family's three generations, covering seventy-five to hundred years, portrays a robust and enduring succession plan?' All shareholders endorsed this 'succession plan' with a thunderous applause.

The Q&A between these two shareholders satisfied me as much as it amused me. Though unknowingly, the second shareholder had provided an accurate and farsighted account of the future of our family-managed business. The captain of our third generation, Athang, was born in January 1992. His birth had brought new hopes and aspirations for our family. For

Kantabai, it was as if Athang had brought paradise on earth.

The company first paid a handsome premium on the equity shares and then floated a rights issue. In just two years thereafter, it came up with a Euro Issue, for which the earlier mentioned gathering was held. The company could accrue a premium of around 90 crore rupees by selling its shares with a face value of 10 rupees at 350 rupees through this issue. The company had established a record.

Kantabai was busy searching for suitable matches for our third and fourth sons, Ajit and Atul, and our nephew, Abhay. As always, my uncle Dalubhau played a lead role in this initiative! I had issued certain guidelines for evaluating the prospective brides who would suit our joint family culture. More importance was to be given to the historical and cultural roots of the family rather than the family's present status. Nobility of the family was to be given preference over their material status. Sanskaar were to be preferred over degrees. High character was to be considered more valuable than good looks. These were some of my guidelines. Matrimonial alliances join two families in lasting bonds, so there should be no undue haste in choosing the right partner. One of the important guidelines was also that any alliance should only be decided after an evaluation and a preliminary waiting period of at least six months.

Kantabai was so agreeable to these guidelines that they became her dictums too. She did not allow even a slight leniency or change in them. After all, my role model while deciding on these guidelines was Kantabai herself! How can any instruction fail, when its inspiration was Kantabai! Time stands testimony to this—all with God's grace.

One thought was predominant among all considerations—the daughters-in-law should take the family to greater glory, not break its integrity and unity. Dalubhau and Kantabai would evaluate all proposals on this primary criterion, and then I would visit the shortlisted families. Further discussions would follow these visits. Then, the two candidates would meet and discuss all aspects freely and fairly. Complete freedom was given to both at this stage to talk and exchange ideas in a democratic atmosphere. We were even prepared to respect the situation where the groom might like the bride, but she may not like him. Luckily, such a situation did not arise.

As foster parents, we had the privilege of performing our niece Anju's kanyadaan. The same parameters that we had established for the selection of a bride applied for the selection of grooms too. In short, all our considerations culminated into one notion—the grooms for our daughters should be superior to them and our daughters-in-law should be superior to our sons! Kantabai was a testimony to this notion; she was superior to me in all respects! We were all very happy that Anju got a noble, well-educated and amiable match. However, she was a bit impulsive and strong-headed, so we were slightly concerned about her.

Anju was very fond of Kantabai. Her anecdotes about Kantabai's participation in the Ladies' Club are very engaging and entertaining. Often, Kantabai would get delayed at the Club's meetings. This would upset her because she wanted to be home when I came for lunch. At times, she would have stepped in just a few minutes before me, but even then she managed everything perfectly. Efficiency was Kantabai's middle name! I would have never come to know about this, had Anju not mentioned it to me recently. A particular episode that one of Kantabai's friends narrated to Anju is very interesting. This lady was very fond of using the phrase, 'Our collar should always be tight' (meaning, we should always be seen as a superior lot) in the Club's meetings. This would puzzle the other ladies as they took it literally and would say, 'How could we ladies have collars?' Kantabai broke her friend's habit in a playful yet effective and amiable manner. During the silver jubilee celebrations of the Club, she called the lady on the stage and gifted her a crisp, stiff collar! Then she made her wear it and praised her, 'Ladies, learn to keep your collars tight like her. We are all distinguished in our own way, so why shouldn't we flaunt it?' Kantabai did this so beautifully! She changed her friend's mannerism so playfully and tactfully, without hurting her ego.

The two decades between 1982 and 2000 were memorable both for the family and for the business. There was an endless series of problems that brought us not only untold hardships, friction and illnesses, but also pain, suffering and sorrow. Certain events that led to colossal losses pushed us to the brink of bankruptcy. But, at the same time, many positive and heartening events brought us happiness and contentment. Many of our wishes came true during this period, and we learnt to fulfill our small and big responsibilities towards one and all.

What did we not get from these two decades? We were gifted with four sons, one after the other, between 1962 and 1969, which is why we were fortunate to be gifted with six grandchildren in the span of seven to eight years. The planning of our family that we had adopted immediately after marriage was now showing results in the form of the timely and opportune branching of our third generation in the family tree. We felt gratified.

Personal and corporate respect as well as recognition was also growing by leaps and bounds. I was bestowed the honorary membership of the Indian Institute of Engineers. Then the FAAI Foundation gave me an award for establishing new landmarks in agriculture and extension services. But the crowning recognition came in the form of the Crawford Reid Award. This is a global benchmark award in the irrigation sector, given by the Irrigation Association, USA. I was the first in India and only the second Asian to receive this award.

At home there was joy with the auspicious entry of my daughters-in-law. Grandchildren followed in due time. May it be granddaughters or grandsons, the pleasure of witnessing our vast family tree growing in front of our eyes was very gratifying. Athang, Amoli, Aashuli, Abhedya, Abhang, Aarohi and now Aatman—were all the Almighty's invaluable gifts to our family. In particular, we were delighted by the arrival of Aatman, because our eldest daughter-in-law, Jyoti, gave birth to him after nineteen years of marriage. She was naturally overjoyed, and that compounded Kantabai's joy infinitely. Aarohi, the first daughter of Ashok and Jyoti, was also born after twelve years of marriage. Kantabai had handled the difficult task of supporting Jyoti during this period very lovingly. As a grandmother, Kantabai had the joy of raising only Athang with her own hands. She 'enjoyed' this privilege to the fullest and showered her love and attention on Athang for over six to seven years. However, she did not overdo it. Her pampering never resulted in spoiling him.

Kantabai had taught an invaluable lesson to everyone in the family: 'Our life is meant to offer something, not to receive anything.' While remembering her mother-in-law, Nisha, my second daughter-in-law and Athang's mother, narrated an incident. Once she had slapped Athang for some mischief or the other. Kantabai immediately took Athang in her arms and gently reprimanded Nisha, 'I do not like my grandchildren to be beaten for any reason. Matters can be handled lovingly, without being harsh to children.' After that day, Nisha stopped even scolding the children, leave aside beating them. However, Kantabai herself had beaten Athang once. She had spanked him on his back. Athang used to bite everyone in his childhood. Kantabai had to beat him to make him get rid of this bad habit. She herself was very pained to punish Athang in this manner, but it was her unpleasant duty to do so. This she had tearfully confided to me later. Only I know the anguish that she had gone through at that time. I marvel at the many roles that Kantabai played in her life expertly—one person, so many dimensions!

Once, the barber was cutting Athang's hair at our Jain Hills bungalow. He was sitting on my shoulders. This bit of play had reduced his crying. After a while, I said to the barber, 'This is enough for today.' However, only one side of Aathang's hair had been cut.

Kantabai took the matter in her own hands and allowed me to go to office. Athang was crying inconsolably at that time. Even I got emotional seeing him sobbing uncontrollably, but Kantabai, the strict disciplinarian, was not moved! She insisted that the barber cut Athang's hair fully then and there, notwithstanding the child's tears. Kantabai was ever careful that indiscipline did not take root in the guise of love and extra care. She never had an argument with anybody as to whose responsibility it was to rectify mistakes. She believed in setting things right herself whenever she felt things were going wrong.

She was always very vigilant about her grandchildren in this matter. She had once observed, 'Athang is Athang and Amoli is Amoli.' Her statement had two distinct dimensions. Firstly, it called for flexibility as far as the bringing up of young boys and girls was concerned. There was a distinct way in which the personality of a boy and a girl had to be moulded. Kantabai possessed abundant experience in this matter. The other dimension was that each child is born with unique individuality. It cannot be presumed that children born to the same mother would bear similar traits. Everyone has his or her distinct characteristics, strengths and weaknesses. It is vital to understand each child's qualities and nurture it accordingly. The more we understand this factor, the better we will be able to mentor our children. Kantabai's rich experience in this matter was very beneficial to our daughters-in-law.

As in every other respect, Kantabai's concern for discipline and the superior upbringing of the grandchildren was born from her deep love for the family. She would always say, 'No matter where we go for vacations, whether to Lonavala, Matheran, Ooty or Rome, my heart will always remain where our home is, in Jalgaon.' She had boundless attachment to her home and all its members. Well, that is what made Kantabai a homemaker and not just a housewife.

We lived in rented houses for twenty-eight years—from 1962 till 1990. Our second daughter-in-law Nisha entered our 'own' home. That is, the house we had purchased. So, all our daughters-in-law except the eldest, Jyoti, entered our 'own' home after marriage. Although these twenty-eight years were very eventful in terms of our progress and success, Kantabai never hassled or nagged me with complaints like, 'We should have been able to purchase our own house a long time back.' At a personal level, I must say that it never occurred to me to buy a house during all those years! I must have been really preoccupied with the priorities of developing a global business from scratch! Besides, whatever money we earned was reinvested in the business. Anyway, for me, it did not matter whether it was a rented house or an owned one. Home for me was where happiness was, or should I say it more accurately, 'Home was where the family's Lakshmi, Kantabai, was.' May God bless every home with a homemaker like Kantabai!

We had started investing in business extensively, using all possible resources. The company's borrowing capacity had multiplied manifold due to the fresh infusion of funds from the rights issue and the Euro issue. We started borrowing aggressively and utilized those funds for the company's growth and diversification. We entered into agreements with seven companies in Israel and several others elsewhere. We embarked upon ambitious diversification and entered into onion dehydration, fruit processing, computers and IT, multimedia, granite mining, finance, etc. In this manner we invested heavily in many businesses that were unrelated to our core activities. We started as many as twelve ventures simultaneously. The list also included the solar energy division. To our singular bad luck, the Indian share market had a major crisis and plummeted down steeply during this time. Some of our ventures, too, followed suit, as we could not provide inspiring leadership. All our planning and homework went haywire. We were heading towards a devastating setback through a fateful mix of circumstances, bad luck and bad decisions. Our credibility took a very heavy beating. Yet, I was clear that we had lost some of our credibility and reputation, but not our character. I issued big advertisements in all the major newspapers of India, openly apologizing for this monumental error of judgment. It was perhaps for the first time in the corporate history of India that a chairman of a large company signed a public apology for his mistakes and thus took all moral and material responsibility. Thus good corporate governance did exist before it was so coined by the contemporary management gurus! This was the only dubious 'first' that we achieved during our darkest days, and it did lift the heavy burden off my conscience.

I had my third heart attack on 30 September 1994 at my residence, Jain House. I had to undergo a second bypass surgery in the US in November the same year. I don't know why, but my self-confidence was badly shaken this time. I called all the company's associates along with their wives for a gathering. I was not sure at all whether I would return, and wanted to bid a farewell to them. I spoke from my heart on that occasion. I told them, 'Friends, this is the first time in the history of this company's thirty years that an occasion to take leave has come. God forbid, if this does happen, you all should not take a day off even on that day. You must remember me through work. I am leaving behind a legacy of a different kind—work instead of wealth, continuous hard work instead of possessions, responsibility instead of indulgence and opulence.' These seemed like my last words even to me, but as fate would have it, I did return.

Kantabai was seated in the front row. She could hide her tears from the world, but not from me. I still remember the heartbroken, 'don't-leave-me' look on her tearful face even today. All her life, hardly anyone had ever seen her cry. She was calmness and composure personified, under every conceivable tragic or stressful situation. I was operated upon in November 1994. Shakuntalabai told me later that Kantabai had wept like a child on the day of the operation. She had indeed felt disoriented and as lost as a helpless child. Her world was on the verge of crumbling; she was utterly helpless in the face of such circumstances. My situation was not any better. I was a shadow of my usual self. My confidence was at its lowest ebb. I was withdrawn and morose, like a man defeated not by challenges, but by fate. Perhaps, it was my pessimistic manner that had caused her rapid demoralization. When a giant of a man falls, for how long can his woman bear the anguish, no matter how strong and resilient she may be. There was a limit to even a sturdy ship's capacity for weathering rough storms.

Because of all these successive setbacks, Kantabai fell gravely ill in 1996. Our problems just kept multiplying. The economic crisis had trapped the company in its vice-like grip. My mother passed away the same year. Even though I was middle aged, I felt like an orphan when mother left us. I was an emotional wreck. 'Whose womb that protected and shaped me for nine months, whose sanskaar moulded me, whose generous heart I inherited—is no more.' I would break down saying this. Kantabai and I felt that the shield that had protected us was gone. We both felt her loss acutely. My cousin Rajendra too, passed away in a fatal car accident in the prime of his youth during this time. His untimely demise shook the whole family. Pain and sorrow, disease and ailments, difficulties and distress, failures and falls—they always come in multitudes. They also come suddenly but leave at leisure.

When the sky ruptures, is there a thread and a needle that can sew it? Incessant catastrophes engulfed us all in profound grief.

Sheila Mayur, Kantabai's friend, once narrated an incident that emphasized Kantabai's presence of mind and genial nature. We were in the US for my surgery. A few days after the surgery, we went to watch a programme in a theatre in Orlando. Both Kantabai and I were given wheelchairs—I, because of my recent surgery, and she, because of her impaired walking. As we were leaving, Kantabai forgot to lock the wheels, and the chair started sliding down the ramp. The American audience watching this debacle thought Kantabai was performing some kind of a stunt, and started cheering! She would have had a really bad fall, had she not managed to lock the wheels in time. Realizing what the people around her were thinking, she did not panic, but smilingly acknowledged their applause! She felt neither embarrassed nor upset by the audience's response to her plight. She did not lose her cool even when the situation was alarming and dangerous. It was Kantabai at her best! To take a joke is infinitely more difficult than to make a joke. Kantabai excelled at the former.

Kantabai was deeply disturbed by my three major heart attacks and the resultant two bypass surgeries. The shocks had levied a heavy toll on her. To add to this, Atul's matrimonial discord increased her miseries. Sometimes, all the caution and careful planning prove ineffectual before destiny's designs. In spite of everything, Atul's marriage could not be salvaged. What does one call such a misfortune? Fate, providence or sheer bad luck? Such jolts in life draw us towards the theory that our lives are after all governed by a higher power. By now, we had become emotionally edgy, our nerves were raw and we felt vulnerable. To tell the truth, Kantabai could never recover fully from this last shock. Atul was her most beloved child, and to see his life being uprooted in front of her eyes, proved to be too much for a mother's heart. Silent suffering ate at her very core.

On the midnight of 14 August 1997, I was addressing a gathering of freedom fighters and some other dignitaries. While sitting down after the speech, I had my fourth heart attack. This time, the attack had the upper hand—I was gone, my heart stopped beating. But for Dr Chaudhary's immediate shock treatment, I would not have survived. Ajit held my jaws wide open so that my breathing was not interrupted. He also breathed into my mouth. Witnessing my 'temporary demise', both Kantabai and Dr Chaudhary's wife, Shardabai, wept inconsolably.

The economic crisis of our business was at its peak. We had almost become bankrupt. Our debt was now larger than our turnover. On the other side, domestic and family problems were also piling up. One of my nieces eloped from home. Our age-old, time-honoured family tradition was broken. Kantabai's heart was like a dam breached at many places by these floods of misfortune. After the attack of August 1997, I suffered my fifth heart attack in January 1998. Here once again Dr Chaudhary's shock treatment saved my life. It seemed as if he was only born to give me a second life! In the twenty-five years between 1982 and 2007, I suffered ten cardiac events including five heart attacks. In eight of these, Dr Chaudhary was either present or could reach my side within ten minutes of the attack. Was this all predestined? Was it the sheer strength of friendship and love that kept him close to me? Or was he returning favours from some earlier life? To be able to know one's heart through non-verbal communication, the accidental coming together of two like-minded persons—this is a part of occult science. Such relationships create bonds that are stronger than blood relations. Sharda Choudhary became my rakhi sister and Dr Chaudhary, Kantabai's rakhi brother. What would Kantabai ask from this brother while tying the rakhi? He had already gifted her her beloved husband's life, many lives, without her asking!

Everyone in the family thought that my frequent cardiac problems were caused because of the economic catastrophe and the breakneck speed of business. The magnitude of the family crises took its toll on Kantabai's health. As if this was not enough, Kantabai's mother passed away in November 1999. Her father had already departed earlier. Kantabai's mother would come and stay with us for a fortnight at least twice a year. Kantabai sorely missed her mother, and this deteriorated her condition further.

We were desperate to save our business. It was a do-or-die situation. We diluted our share value by half. We had to stop our Papain plant after twenty-five years of its successful operation. We also had to terminate all the agreements that were made between 1995 and 2000. The business world, particularly amongst the financial circles, was unanimous in their opinion that not even the Almighty could save this company and this family. Our lives had been an endless saga of toil and struggle. Passing through all the good and bad times, successes and failures, darkness and light, the doomsday had arrived and we were now standing on the edge of an abyss, staring at its bottomless depth. Kantabai's neurological ailment was advancing gradually. First, she started losing control over her movements. Then she almost totally lost her speech. She could not even feed herself. The Annapurna of our family now had to be fed by her daughters-in-law. She started needing help in dressing herself too. She had become totally dependent on others. Once a personification of high spirits and perpetual enthusiasm, Kantabai was now withdrawn and gloomy. Her gaze was fixed and empty. She would watch the world pass her by with hollow, vacant eyes. Her intellectual and emotional faculties were fully active, but she had lost her expression.

What can I say about her health prior to this ailment? In all the thirty-five years from 1961 to 1995–96, she did not suffer from even minor ailments like coughs and colds. She had never needed medicines or injections, and except during childbirth, had never been hospitalized. She had just one problem of an impaired knee from the injury related earlier, but that had no remedy. She had reconciled to this lifelong impairment. Earlier, Dr Subhash Chaudhary and I took Kantabai to Mumbai to consult the renowned neurologist, Dr Wadia. After his investigation in 1995–96, he pronounced, 'Her nerves are like gold.' Then, when I took her to Chennai for treatment at Apollo Hospital, the diagnosis was more or less the same; her overall health was good. After returning from Chennai, I started taking personal interest in Kantabai's caretaking. The family was relieved and had become positive about Kantabai's health after the encouraging diagnosis. Everybody believed that she would come out of her ailment soon, aided by the medicines and the loving care of all the family members. We also started treating her with alternative therapies like yoga, meditation, acupressure, acupuncture, ayurveda, aromatherapy and even religious discourses and devotional music. We followed whatever suggestions we received from people in order to improve Kantabai's health. Apart from respecting everybody's opinion, our basic objective was not to leave any stone unturned in treating her. She had already been referred to every known neurologist in India. Moreover, we also sent Dr Chaudhary to a world-renowned research institute in Washington, DC, along with her complete case history. However, no hope was forthcoming from anywhere.

When we got Kantabai's MRI done at Jaslok Hospital in 1999, it was found that her brain had a swelling which was bound to increase with time. In 1996, we had received a similar indication from Dr SM Katrak. He had also said that the swelling would not remain localized but would gradually affect the cells in the entire brain. The ailment was at an early stage then (1996), but even then he had said that it was untreatable. But I was not the one to give up so easily. In spite of knowing her predicament, I tried all the treatments mentioned above. Above all, her best treatment was the 24/7 love and care given by the family and the concern shown by all.

The company's condition continued to be extremely critical. But suddenly, there was a ray of hope. My son Anil, who is the managing director of the company, received an email from a gentleman named Anup Jacob. He represented an investment fund in the US. He had visited the company's stall at the exhibition organized by the Irrigation Association, USA. Thereafter he had also studied our website and then had written to us.

Our fund has a narrow focus on water-related companies. We invest only in these companies. We have studied Jain Irrigation's website and are convinced that, prima facie, it is the type of company we would like to invest in. We are keen to discuss the matter. Kindly contact me.

Considering our dire state, this was a god-sent opportunity. We ourselves could not believe that anybody would risk bailing us out. We had been practically written off.

Anil discussed the matter with me on the phone and immediately conveyed our willingness to Anup Jacob in the US. A long trail of discussions followed, and ultimately Aqua International of the US announced its 49.4 per cent stake in Jain Irrigation in August 2002. It promptly invested 183 crore rupees in the company. The company's share was priced around 37 rupees at that time, which they bought at 77.37 rupees.

However, this rescue package came at a cost. We had to agree to humiliating terms while entering into the final deal. It belittled us in the market. But it was we who needed them. We did not have any option but to accept their strangulating terms. We lost our majority on the Board of the company. We could not spend even 50 lakh rupees without their consent. We were expected to run at breakneck speed to turn the company around, but with shackles on. We had surrendered our independence. We signed on the dotted line with a lump in our throats.

The brighter side of the deal was that we could repay most of our debt with this freshly infused money. Thereafter, each one of us got busy saving our sinking ship with renewed vigour and enthusiasm. We embarked upon a takeover spree. We bought many sick units at 30 to 35 per cent of their original price. These included the onion and vegetable dehydrating units in Dindori (Nashik) and Baroda, and a fruit-processing unit in Hyderabad.

We also began production of solar PV cells in 2003–04.

In the meantime, Kantabai once again became instrumental in providing the opportunity for a reunion of the entire Jain family. Our Kuldevta (family deity) Sachhiyayji Mata's shrine is situated at Oshia near Jodhpur in Rajasthan. It was customary for every newlywed couple in our community to visit that shrine and offer obeisance. However, both my brother Kantilal and I had missed abiding by this custom for some reason or the other. Since we, as family heads, had missed performing this ritual, our children were also not able to undertake this pilgrimage after their marriages. My parents had performed this puja and hence we were expected to perform it too. In fact, they had expressed their wish time and again that we do so. Kantabai, too, was always reminding me, but somehow we could not go to Oshia. Some thing or the other, work priorities, children's school schedules always hindered our plans to make this visit.

Kantabai had told me three months prior to Deepavali, 'I know I am not well enough to undertake the long journey to Oshia, but I earnestly desire to go there. Please fulfill my wish.'

It was decided to use the Deepavali holidays for the Oshia pilgrimage. Initially, it was planned that Kantilal's and my families would undertake the pilgrimage. However, Kantabai asked Ashok, 'Why don't we take the entire extended Jain family with us? Is it possible to do so?' Ashok asked me. I was overwhelmed with emotion on hearing her request. Kantabai knew she was nearing the end of her journey. It was almost like her final wish to see the entire family together one last time. Who was I to say no? Her wish was my command.

I undertook every task with proper planning. A comprehensive list of the tour members was prepared. Our family was now 125-strong! The youngest member was the three-month old daughter of our nephew Avinash, and the eldest was our eighty-five-year old paternal uncle (Phuphaji), Bansilalji. Ashok and Atul meticulously planned the entire tour. They poured their hearts into it. They deserve all the credit for the tour's 'historical' success.

Kantabai was extremely happy throughout the tour. The jumbo-sized family mingled and converged into a rainbow of happy harmony. There were 125 individuals, but it was just one big family. There was much joking and plenty of leg-pulling. Long hours of cozy chats filled the chilly evenings with heartfelt contentment. Seeing her family immersed in such joy, made Kantabai's heart upbeat. Her happiness reached a climax when we performed the puja of Sachhiyayji Mata. It was a rare moment for her. One of her most ardent wishes; rather, her final wish was being fulfilled. Festive meals were arranged for our entire sub-caste before going to the temple and after coming back. Auspicious gifts were distributed to all family members along with the prasadam (the offerings of food items made to the deity).

Seeing the family so happy made us very happy. Our joy was immeasureable, beyond any expression of words. I wondered then, what would she have prayed for before the deity? Undoubtedly, her fervent prayer would have been that the family remains united in numbers, undivided at heart and happy forever.

I remember well that it was Kantabai who had started the custom of gathering the entire family, just like this on every Rakshabandhan day. If one desires to experience the joys of a joint family multiplied by 'n', then one also has to work towards keeping its integrity and unity intact. 'She' and 'Me' were viewing this infinitely happy journey from this angle. It was an incomparable, unforgettable family tour.

Many of our family members came to know and understand

each other better during this tour. Many new bonds were established, and the existing ones became stronger. Our four generations met and came closer during this journey. The older generation passed on the torch of togetherness to the younger generation. Unity and integrity of the family thus got passed from the past to the present. That is why this family tour amounted to more than a joyous vacation; it became a journey towards solidarity and unity.

∞

We were recovering lost ground in business rapidly. We bought Terra Agro, a Tamil Nadu-based company with 1,200 acres of agricultural land and a dehydration unit. In our Jalgaon fruit-processing plant, we added the IQF (Instant Quick Frozen) facility. Our shares zoomed to around 160 rupees and stabilized there. Just seven to eight years back, their value had dwindled to less than 10 rupees per share. We could feel that destiny was smiling upon us again.

On 2 September 2005, Aqua ceased to be our shareholders. They were glad to exit our company with a 100 per cent return on their investment within just three years. We regained our independence.

Meanwhile, my romance with heart attacks continued. I had one more in 2003, which came and went. Then, a paralytic attack joined the long queue of 'attacks' in 2004. It seemed as if all these attacks were ganging up against me and threatening me, 'Oh man you better beware of us. How long will you keep eluding us? We will catch up with you one day soon.' My last two attacks occurred during Kantabai's serious illness, and they compounded her agony.

Kantabai led every family initiative with high enthusiasm. She was the one to lead by example. She donned the role of

Annapurna not only for the family but also for everybody who was hungry. She gave herself to me unconditionally in every act of passion and thus made it a divine experience of utmost satisfaction. She gave her very best for the sake of family, community, society and religion. She was second to only mother Earth in generosity, resilience and forgiveness. In countless ways, Kantabai would top the list of ideal homemakers who deserve these superlatives.

19

TERRA AGRO WAS set up by an accomplished industrialist from Coimbatore. He had done so, not so much because he was convinced that it would work, but because he loved his only son and wanted to indulge his whims and wishes. The son had strived very hard for two-three years to establish and turn the unit around. He had also earned a good reputation for the project. The capital investment itself was around 60–65 crore rupees, not counting the interest. We bought it for just 12–13 crores. We had also bought similar sick units at throwaway prices. In short, Jain Irrigation was totally out of the red by then. It had risen from the ashes of its debacle between 1996 and 2001 like the proverbial phoenix. Just as we had to sell our invaluable assets for a pittance during that time, we also bought other units in the same manner. Providence had balanced the credit and debit sides of our fate.

For Kantabai, it had become routine to bear my long absences from home. I had made it a point to revive the sick units that we had purchased under my personal supervision. When I told her that I was going to be in Udumalpet for some time, she gladly gave her consent, 'Go, but return early.' Perhaps, this was an indication whose implication I had failed to decode at that time.

I was engaged in an animated discussion with the company associates. Although the fan was on and the room was adequately ventilated by its north-east facing windows, I was feeling uneasy. As if to confirm my ominous premonition, Ashok called up,

'Bhau, you better leave immediately for Jalgaon. Bai's condition has suddenly become very critical. We have already arranged for a chartered plane for you from Hyderabad. It will get you to Aurangabad in two to two-and-half hours. You will have to travel from Aurangabad to Jalgaon by road. You will be here by ten or twelve in the night.' Ashok could not control himself while talking. I, too, was shaken, but realizing Ashok's condition, I tried to console him, 'You don't worry, I am reaching there… Nothing untoward will happen.'

A storm of thoughts and emotions raged through my mind. Her love for her sons and for me was so profound that I had always taken it for granted that she will never leave us; she would not leave before me in any case, that had remained my firm conviction throughout life.

I had given her whatever I had. Likewise, she had submitted everything that was hers to me. We were no longer separate in any sense. We had always prayed for the children, borne out of our union, to be better than us. While travelling through life, we had learned from each other that oneness of hearts is greater than oneness of bodies. The track that led to that summit of sublime companionship was treacherous, but having reached there, the effort seemed nothing compared to the rewards. To meditate on that summit, to become ego-less before each other, to become worry-free in each other's company, to let go of all sense of individuality and to drift effortlessly in the sea of togetherness hand-in-hand, and finally, to come to the sublime realization that the companionship was now so strong that it will transcend this life and continue in the next—this is as near as I can get to express the kind of inexpressible togetherness that existed between 'She' and 'Me'.

This realization did not come suddenly like a flash of lightening. Rather, it developed in our married lives almost imperceptibly, but steadily. Our bonds became stronger and stronger. Love changes its outer manifestation at different stages of our life. However, love remains love throughout.

She came in as my wife. She became the mother of our children and ultimately, before her departure, she was like a mother to me.

The above is my honest depiction of what happened between her and me. Can psychology, parapsychology or science attempt to explain this phenomenon? Was it not just 'sublime sense' operating here? I do not want to enter into the realms of any limiting definitions.

She had become very fragile, both mentally and physically.

I was lost in the bylanes of memory as I looked out at the dull, monochrome sky from the plane's window. Suddenly, I started feeling breathless. I had to intermittently use oxygen from the bottle that we had brought along. But it was over within an hour. When I asked for more oxygen, the flight attendant cautioned, 'We have very limited supply. Please use it very sparingly.' Aurangabad was another sixty to ninety minutes away. I was already swaying between life and death. An ominous thought flashed through my mind. If Kantabai's departure is predestined this time, what is wrong if I too join her in her onward journey? But at the very next moment, the faces of my sons and daughters-in-law, grandchildren, friends and associates in the company appeared before my eyes. I regained my wavering mental balance. This was not the time to give in to such emotions. I had to remain here; if not for myself, then for the sake of my family and friends, and for the sake of countless farmers of my motherland who were living in abject poverty. Did I not owe them a better life? Was my duty limited to only my family, friends and associates? I willed myself forcefully to think positively, that Kantabai will not leave yet, I will not let her leave.

Dr Chaudhary called just as I landed at Aurangabad airport, 'Bhau, Bai is not yet out of danger, but slightly better. She may further improve after you reach here.'

I reached Jalgaon and entered the ICU room. Locking my eyes with hers even though hers were shut, I placed my hand on her forehead. Then, I too shut my eyes tightly. I delved deep within myself, extracted every bit of energy from within me, channelled it to my palms and transmitted it to her. Kantabai's eyes flickered after two-three minutes, as if to acknowledge my presence. However, she kept slipping in and out of consciousness. Her breathing too was erratic.

Kantabai's already acute condition had deteriorated because some morsels of food had entered her windpipe while being fed. This had played havoc and had led to multiple problems. The resulting rampant infection remained uncontrolled in spite of all efforts. As we know, hospital infections are nasty; they are easy to contract but difficult to get rid of.

All the doctors were extremely vigilant and were burning the midnight oil, but there was no perceptible improvement in Kantabai's condition. It was not advisable and certainly risky to shift her to Mumbai in that condition. In the meantime, the crowd of relatives and well-wishers was swelling day by day at Sahyog Critical Hospital where Kantabai was admitted. Only a few people were allowed to enter her ICU room. But even in that critical condition, she was not lax in showing courteousness. If she happened to be awake and conscious when an elderly relative visited her, she remembered to cover her head with her sari as a mark of respect.

On the matter of relationships, I would like to bring in an old incident. Readers will remember that I had suffered from jaundice after my LLB exams in Nashik. Dr Doshi, who was then the medical superintendent of Nashik jail, had affectionately insisted that we stay at his home for the period of my recuperation. When my paternal cousin Girdhari came to see me, I introduced him to Kantabai as my maternal cousin. She was quick to respond, 'How come he is your maternal uncle's son when you don't have a maternal uncle?' I quickly corrected my mistake. I concede that I am poor at accurately remembering the complex relationships within the large extended family. Notwithstanding this weakness, I was never found wanting in maintaining the relationships per se. However, Kantabai always remained two steps ahead of me in this respect. Decades later, when Girdhari's daughter was getting married, Kantabai still remembered the courtesy that he had shown by visiting us then. She lovingly knitted a pair of socks for Girdhari's daughter as her special marriage gift. What is incredible about this incident is that Kantabai had taken up knitting after twenty-seven years! I view those socks as a manifestation of the warmth and affection with which she had knitted and nurtured precious bonds not only in our large joint family, but also in the much larger extended family which had branched out far and wide. She had spent her whole life nurturing countless blood relations.

The orchard of our family was lush and full of fruit, thanks to Kantabai's single-minded devotion and care. She did possess a deep, instinctive understanding of how to maintain relations, which I lacked. She was ever watchful of the finer details when it came to maintaining relations. For example, a certain relative may be younger in age, but senior in status. She would remember all this, which was beyond me. If I respect a person, I respect him, notwithstanding his age or his status. This was my simple equation in life.

According to me, there are only two types of people: the ones whom you like and the ones whom you don't. And no matter how hard we try to be free of bias, our behaviour and attitude towards them does reflect the extent of our liking for them. But Kantabai had different criteria for evaluation. She approached every relation with fairness and equality, irrespective of the fact whether she liked the relative or not. In contrast, I would tend to be preferential towards the ones whom I was fond of, and ignore the ones whom I found less amicable.

This inherent weakness of mine was more than made up for by Kantabai's fair conduct. Together, we were able to do things almost faultlessly. The outsiders never came to know about our weaknesses, imperfections or handicaps. She complemented me and I complemented her perfectly as a couple. We always steered clear of the perceived need of having separate individual 'spaces' in our combined life.

It had been a fortnight since Kantabai was admitted to Sahyog Critical Hospital. It was not that her condition did not improve at all during that time. She could breathe on her own without the help of the ventilator for seven to eight hours a day. This improvement came as a great relief for all of us. Our anxiety was reduced to an extent.

A heartening thought came to all of us. What if we moved Kantabai home? After all, a familiar hospital, despite all its facilities, can never substitute the familiar comfort of a homely atmosphere. This was especially true for Kantabai, for whom home meant her whole universe. She had never felt comfortable for more than a few days in any other place than her home. She had transformed a brick and mortar house into a home that was built on the firm foundation of love, care and happiness. For her, to be confined in a hospital room for long would indeed be unbearable. We all were eager to free her and take her home.

I, who had always had a final say in every matter, was for once indecisive on this. I was satisfied with the facilities at the hospital and so was a bit sceptical whether such an immaculate ICU setup could be created at home. Besides these facilities, round-the-clock vigilance and professional care were also of vital importance. The whole thought required serious multidimensional consideration. One small oversight or inadequacy could prove fatal. For the first time in their lives, my four sons came up with a bold, unanimous opinion, 'Bhau, today you please endorse whatever we say. We need just your nod to take Bai home. Everything else will fall in place. We will establish a world-class ICU at home. We will give it whatever it takes.'

The task was undertaken on a war footing. Round-the-clock work began immediately to convert an adjoining two-storeyed guesthouse into a state of the art, ultramodern ICU of international standards. Ajit took it upon himself to procure all the required equipment within just two-three days. He resolved to buy only the best and the latest in the world. On the other hand, Ashok busied his core team from the food-processing unit in thoroughly fumigating and disinfecting the house. A task force of experts from diverse disciplines like engineers, architects, food specialists, air-conditioning specialists, etc, was formed and they began their work simultaneously.

Normally, it takes at least a week to import a world-class ventilator. This was not acceptable to Ajit. So, he procured the demonstration piece available with the Indian dealer. The installation of the entire ventilator system was also undertaken as an emergency.

An expert medical team was sourced immediately for Kantabai's 24-hour treatment and care. Two medical specialists and two to three experienced nurses were hired from Mumbai and Pune. They were provided excellent accommodation on the ground floor of the house. The latest and most sophisticated facilities for their rest, recreation and living-dining areas were also provided.

Within a few days, a world-class ICU setup was ready. The task would have taken a few months for others, but my four sons did it in just a few days. They wanted to bring home their mother, for whom home was where her family was.

Usually, it was Kantabai who stood at the doorstep to receive me. On 29 June 2005, it was I who anxiously awaited her return from the hospital. When she came, her eyes glittered with the joy of homecoming. She was perhaps thinking, 'Now whatever happens, it will happen at home.'

The dos and don'ts of the hospital were no more applicable at home. Moreover, since the ICU was fitted with CCTV cameras, even those who could not meet Kantabai in person could see her from outside. Minute-to-minute monitoring of the ICU was available outside. There was no need for everyone to visit the ICU to 'meet' Kantabai. In spite of the nurses attending to her round-the-clock, the four daughters-in-law had decided among themselves to be present by Kantabai's side in eight-hour shifts—24/7.

Despite all these facilities and care, Kantabai's total incapacitation tore at our hearts. She, who was a fountainhead of energy and enthusiasm, who had raised the grandchildren like her own children, who had catered to their every wish and demand, and had consoled and comforted them in her lap day and night—now could not even speak a word to them, or touch them lovingly, or lift them up with gleeful affection.

Kantabai's helplessness and dependence raised a storm of emotions in our hearts. We desperately wanted to do something for her, but could do nothing except watch her helplessness helplessly! There was nothing we could do but to submit to circumstances. Confidence and hopefulness both were lost. I was totally powerless before the situation, and could do nothing more than stoically suffer the continuous emotional ordeal. I may have looked composed from the outside, but I was in shambles inside. A wall of glass separated my third generation and me from Kantabai, who had been the bridge, the 'common factor' between all the generations in our family.

Although Kantabai could not speak, she expressed her gratitude towards all those who visited her through her expressive eyes. In large families like ours, welcoming and attending to the constant stream of guests on such occasions becomes a full-time job in itself. Everyone who visited us during those days was overwhelmed by the extent of facilities and the sophistication of the ICU.

The officials of the charitable educational institution at Chandwad had come down specially to see Kantabai. My uncle Dalubhau was a trustee there, so they were talking with him after seeing Kantabai. During their talks, the officials presented a spontaneous proposal to us. They expressed their wish to name the engineering college they had established after Kantabai. They incidently referred to a figure of around 30 lakh rupees. Dalubhau accepted the idea heartily and instantly announced a donation of rupees 31 lakh. However, my sons unanimously felt that this amount would be too low. They suggested the figure of rupees 51 lakhs to me. I nodded, and the donation was raised accordingly. The officials were overwhelmed with this gesture of goodwill. They prayed and wished that these worthy sons of a worthy mother would take their parents' name to even greater glory in the future. This college, which has come up at the cost of over rupees 13 crore, proudly bears the name: 'Late Kantabai Bhavarlal Jain College of Engineering', and produces a promising breed of talented engineers.

Although Kantabai had lost her speech, her memory, hearing

and sight were in perfect order. We all knew how suffocated she felt because of her inability to speak. Ashok and Atul had already trained themselves to make out what their mother wanted to say. Where there is a will, there is a way. My family had devised various methods on how to understand Kantabai's unspoken wishes. These included a touch screen monitor, slate and pencil, a plateful of Hindi alphabet letters and numbers, etc. It was very trying and time-consuming to apply these methods and learn what Kantabai's wishes were. But steadfastness, patience and persistent efforts in order to achieve the desired results were our family hallmarks. I was confident that the sons would soon be able to decode the mysteries of their mother's non-verbal communication.

The experiment with Hindi alphabets remained the most successful. The 'method' invented was ingenious. The children would first guess Kantabai's wish and then think of an appropriate word that best 'captured' her wish. They would then point at the first letter of the word, and if Kantabai nodded, they would proceed to the second letter. If the full word received Kantabai's approval, they would then evolve several hypothetical questions based on the clue that the selected word provided. Each question would then be asked to Kantabai, and further probing would be done on the one she said yes to. This communication process was 'mastered' by my eldest daughter-in-law, Jyoti, and some others in a few days. The process was indeed lengthy. Sometimes, it required many hours of interaction with Kantabai to arrive at a conclusion. The importance of a faculty is felt only after losing it—sight after blindness. We normally gauge the worth of legs from the footwear or trousers that covers them. We envy those legs that wear the costliest footwear, and blindly try to copy them. But we only realize the true worth of legs when we see and experience the tribulations of a lame person. Rather, the complete worth of legs is known only to the handicapped. Those who take these natural gifts for granted will probably never realize their vital importance unless they experience such adverse conditions. We were now acutely missing the value of Kantabai's words when she was bereft of them. It is indescribable how overjoyed we felt to communicate with her in some way or the other.

After some time, the children started asking her direct questions, thus cutting short the communication process. The first question would invariably be regarding the home and family. If she responded negatively, the next question would be regarding relatives and other matters. If Kantabai nodded, then a string of connected hypothetical questions would be asked. In order to reconfirm her answer, Ashok and Atul would repeat the question and ask, 'Bai this is what you want to say, right?' They would then ask her to say yes or no by closing her eyes or shaking her head. Often, we could decipher a lot from her facial expressions alone.

This process became near perfect in a short time. Kantabai's debilitated body lay prone, but her mind opened up before us and her wishes could be known just as well as when she was able to speak. The other members also started 'conversing' with Kantabai in this manner. When I watched the success of this experiment, my love and appreciation for the children multiplied.

I feel overcome with emotion even today when I remember that vulnerable period and the much needed emotional support Ashok gave me. His gentle touch and comforting words were like balm for my bruised heart. Children do possess that knack to know the minds of their parents.

Ashok narrated an incident pertaining to that phase, 'My wife Jyoti was reminiscing about Kantabai one day. Kantabai was fond of tea. Her face would light up at the mention of the very word 'tea'. Once Nisha asked her, "Bai do you want anything?" and started showing her the Hindi alphabet letters. Kantabai nodded when the letters making up the word "tea" were shown to her. Then it was reconfirmed, "Do you want tea?" She nodded again. Tea was offered to her after the doctor's consent, but she wanted it for its flavour and taste, meaning that she did not want the tea to be fed through the feeding tubes!'

Another incident from that period—Dalubhau's seventy-third birthday was coming up on 20 August 2005. He was a very straightforward and god-fearing person and his life was guided by humility and simplicity as per the principles of Jainism. He had already given up wearing luxurious or expensive clothing. Leave aside any expensive gold jewellery, he did not even wear a wrist watch. Notwithstanding Dalubhau's pledge, Kantabai wished to give him a gold chain for his birthday. She knew that he would most likely refuse the gift, since she was younger than him, nevertheless she persisted. And to everybody's surprise, Dalubhau not only accepted the gold chain, but also wore it! Kantabai's wish prevailed over his lifelong pledge. Why? Because she had nurtured the relationship so lovingly that it was impossible for anybody to break her heart by saying no. Kantabai also called my younger brother Kantilal and his wife Shakuntalabai and made them sit beside her. Kantabai and Shakuntalabai shared a very affectionate sisterly relationship. Since Kantilal is younger than Kantabai, she authoritatively told him, 'Take good care of her after me. Get some good gold ornaments made for her too.' Kantabai's concern filled everyone's hearts. At the same time, it gave a deeply troubling inkling to everybody; Kantabai had already got the indication that she was nearing the end of her journey.

Kantabai's only medium of expression was her eyes, and to

some extent, her face. We took solace from the fact that at least we were able to know her wishes through the communication method devised by my children. Her every wish was met instantaneously. Ashok and Jyoti were constantly by her side. One by one, she had expressed her wish to give something or the other to everybody—she kept giving until the end! The daughters-in-law, sisters-in-law, nephews and nieces, uncles and aunts, the elders, the boys, the girls, the grandchildren—she did not miss out anybody. Moreover, apart from our relations, she did not forget her obligations even towards our ancestral village, Agolai in Rajasthan. According to her wish, a permanent arrangement for food and water were to be made at the dovecote of the village. Thus, she gave even to the mute birds! She specially remembered the medical team and other associated people who had cared for her day and night. It was not material gifts that she was giving out. She was distributing and sharing her love, compassion and generosity for the last time.

Ashok could make out from his conversations with Kantabai that she was deeply worried and pained on two accounts—one was my heart problem and the other was Atul's remarriage. On the first matter, she was satisfied with the personal care I was taking and the health and medical regime that I was following. But she was not at all satisfied about Atul's future in spite of my repeated assurances that he would get remarried. It was now a year since Atul's marriage had broken up, but even then he was not mentally prepared to marry again. The matter was obviously of grave concern for Kantabai. Ashok and Jyoti had also tried to convince her on this matter, but in vain. Reassurances from many others including Dalubhau failed to satisfy Kantabai. In the end, Ashok asked her, 'Do you want the assurance from Atul himself?' She immediately responded in positive. Atul then went to her and reassured her that he would remarry soon.

Contentment at last welled up in Kantabai's eyes and we felt relieved that her nagging worry was over.

Kantabai's condition continued to worsen day by day. She was in continuous misery. We all longed to see even a hint of a smile on her face. Ashok narrated one more touching incident that occurred during those days. Jyoti, Dr Pendse and some others were chatting in the ICU with Kantabai. Dr Pendse asked her, 'Bai, which doctor do you like the most?' Then he took the names of Dr Subhash Choudhary and Dr Shekhar Raisoni who were always in constant touch, but Kantabai did not respond. Dr Doshi's name was also mentioned, but there was no response. Ultimately, Dr Pendse uttered his name, but Kantabai still remained noncommittal. In the end, Jyoti asked jokingly, 'Is it Dr Bhavarlal Jain whom you like the most?' And Kantabai was quick to bob her head! Everybody burst out laughing heartily. Kantabai's face also lit up with an impish smile. In spite of being in the throes of unbearable pain and suffering, she could make people laugh. As for her devotion to her soulmate, she did not forget to acknowledge this even at a time like this.

∽

Jain Irrigation's partnership with Aqua International ceased to exist on 2 September 2005. Kantabai was informed about this development. She was already aware about Aqua's 183 crore-rupees investment in our company. When asked whether she remembered this, she nodded. Then Ashok updated her that the company had achieved a turnaround and had regained its prestige in the market, thanks to everybody's relentless hard work and dedication. Taking the benefit of this resurgence, Aqua had sold its shares in the open market at rupees 155 per share. They earned 100 per cent profit in just three years and exited Jain Irrigation. We had regained total managerial control. We were once again independent. When Ashok explained all this to Kantabai, her contented expression radiated joy and pride.

Although Kantabai's speech was lost, her hearing was intact; she could receive and comprehend all communication. Her eyes brimmed with undying enthusiasm, self-confidence and desire to live on, despite her incapacitation. That is why I nurtured the illusion in my mind that she will be with me for a long time; that she won't desert me yet.

'She' and 'Me' had merged with each other and become 'Us' soon after our marriage. The water of Bijapur had mixed with the water of Jalgaon and had become forever inseparable. The current of this water was calm, serene and dependable like that of a perennial river, not restive and impulsive like that of a seasonal spring. I had been deeply introspective during those early days of our marriage. Was our union circumstantial to our exterior and material assets like beauty, charm, intellect and affluence? Was it formed on the basis of our likes and dislikes, our worldly and mundane aspirations and our physical needs? Was it related to mutual necessities of the past? Did we live keeping a safe distance between each other? Was our married life dominated by individual egos? Like 'She' is 'She' and 'Me' is 'I'? My introspection went on and on.

The obvious answers were an emphatic 'No'. Our domesticity blossomed to idealistic dimensions very naturally and effortlessly. Nothing was artificially induced, pretentious or thrust upon in our union. There was no duality. There was no separateness in our thoughts. We had therefore dreamed and aspired together, and built common goals. These goals became our aims, and their fulfillment became the fundamental purpose of our lives. That is why, the computations and permutations on which many couples base their domestic life today, just did not apply to us. Our love and affection kept growing and scaling newer heights and achieving deeper dimensions. We had forgotten that we ever existed individually. Our faith and religion, our belief and conviction, even our God had become one. Our sanskaar of selflessness helped us experience the metaphysical aspect of our relationship every new day.

Our overall condition had improved steadily ever since Kantabai entered our home as its Grihalakshmi. Our family and our business flourished after she came into our lives. It is indeed strange that from 1962 to 1996, Kantabai's health was perfectly fine. Our business activities and material wellness also reached new heights during that period. It was almost as if lady luck had decided to lodge permanently in our home. We succeeded in whatever we did; our ventures appeared to have a Midas touch. However, as Kantabai's health deteriorated between 1996 and 2002, our business too followed suit. Jain Irrigation went through historical lows during that time. The company's situation did improve after that, but unfortunately, Kantabai's health did not. She kept declining physically, like a flame gradually flickering out. Why was it so? Nobody could understand destiny's mysterious design. I kept thinking about this deeply disturbing 'why'.

Kantabai's sudden stumbling and falling on the footpath of Kowloon after 1990; then her leg injury on the bridge of the Paldhi River in 1993; the involuntary, but forceful banging of her hand on my chest one night in 1995; the diagnosis of the swelling in her brain in 1996; her growing apathy thereafter and her progressive debility; her increasing difficulty in swallowing food from 2000 onwards, and her stammering—were successive disabilities that all pointed to her rapidly deteriorating health. The doctors had explained that Kantabai's ailment was hereditary. Perhaps that is why she failed to respond to the medical treatment. But notwithstanding all this, she steadfastly and courageously fought against these herculean odds. She defied excruciating pain and insurmountable limitations for five long years. The best ICU facilities and medical care, the ever-competent doctors and caregiving staff, and above all, the heartfelt love of the members of our joint and extended family, which had been nurtured by her painstakingly throughout her life, provided an anchor to her ebbing spirits. They gave her the emotional strength to put up a brave fight. She somehow managed to be with her loved ones until 2005.

If one looks back on Kantabai's last decade, then one cannot escape the feeling that destiny had been unfair to her. She had spent her entire life not only for the good of the family, but also for the welfare of everybody who came into contact with her. She was like a river, a metaphor for life itself. She spread joy, contentment, peace and harmony with her elixir of life. She travelled the toughest and the roughest terrains to create fertile riverbeds on both sides. She emptied herself to enrich the lives of others.

Then, what right had destiny to trouble her in such a manner. This perplexing question puzzled everyone around Kantabai. Nobody had a clue as to why. But I did. In her last act of supreme sacrifice and selflessness, she had sought to take on all my wrongdoings, my faults and follies, my mistakes and injustices before the Almighty and plead with him that 'She' be punished for them, not 'Me'. And at that time, seeing her genuineness, God must have readily obliged. Her prayer that she be called before her time, and that her remaining time be awarded to me, was answered. I know that this may sound overly emotional and therefore irrational, but I have read it in her eyes during her last days. Therefore, I would rather be called emotional and irrational here.

It is said that good acts cannot square off one's bad acts.

There is no such credit and debit facility in God's book of accounts. Neither can good acts be transferred from one account to another. But Kantabai's prayer was fervent. It had emerged from the purest core of her pure heart. When she pleaded with God, 'Let me bear all the pain and suffering, let me die for him! But you please give him a long and happy life', even the Almighty was helpless and had to make an exception in this case.

Was Kantabai's supreme dedication and devotion to me one-sided? Was it that I had manipulated her gullible mind and misused my intellectual and argumentative prowess to thrust that devotion down her throat? Was her devotion a product of the male-dominated society? Or was it a natural outcome of the-then prevalent sociocultural set-up? Worse, was her devotion the surrender in disguise of a helpless and submissive lady?

Countless people had met and interacted with Kantabai during her life. They had asked her many questions in this regard. They had tried to probe her mind and psyche with their analytical and insightful minds. But could arrive at only one conclusion. The genesis of her devotion and dedication was in her sanskaar, her cultural DNA. It was her conscious, willing and heartfelt choice to be the way she was. It was a choice made by her own volition, not by compulsion! And as far as my experience of her is concerned, she had responded to her inner voice while devoting herself to me. Her choice was like a self-adorned ornament; only, it beautified her from within. She never ever felt burdened by it. She had made her choice effortlessly and naturally, just as a hero would choose martyrdom. It was her sterling character that was responsible for her choice. There comes a moment in everybody's life when you succumb to attraction. The rest of the moments in life are meant for the care and concern of each other. Her adoption of this rather simple principle in life created all the 'space' that was needed to nurture our love life. Obviously, the concept of 'space' never occurred, leave alone bothered us.

I became introspective and contemplative while attending to her in those final days.

Her lips would start fluttering as soon as we asked her to recite the Navkaar Mantra (a sacred chant of Jains). She also tried to answer every question that was asked to her, but not everybody could decipher what she said. Leave aside the others; it had become impossible for me too to comprehend what she was trying to say. As her last duty, she had transferred the responsibility of domesticity to Jyoti by virtue of her being the eldest daughter-in-law. It was probably because Jyoti easily understood what she was trying to say in those last days.

20

KANTABAI DRAGGED HER fragile and weak hand to the edge of the bed with much effort. She gestured something to me with her eyes, but I could not understand her. Ashok was standing beside me. He asked her, 'Are you trying to say something? What do you want to do? What is it that you are trying to tell us by your hand movement? Is your hand paining? Or has something happened to it? Or is it that you want to call the grandchildren?' A flurry of questions came out of Ashok's mouth.

All possible questions were put to her, but she neither moved her lips, nor did she nod. Her eyes had gone still, blank and empty. In that fleeting moment, Jyoti understood it all. Gently, she asked her, 'Do you want to touch Bhau's feet?' A trickle instantly started running down from her brimming eyes.

She was seeking my permission to leave. It was as if she was saying, 'My call has come. Please let me go.' But I could not let her do that. How could I? I stood there motionless. I, who had travelled the whole world, could not move closer and cover that short distance. For once, I was unable to reach out to her when she called me. Ultimately, she had to leave without my permission. Her beautiful eyes then shut forever.

The moment had suddenly arrived. The grief that was slowly building up inside finally found its way through tears. And the tears were uncontrollable.

Normally, thunderstorms don't occur in Jalgaon in September. But this one did, on 6 September 2005. It was an unseasonal storm, just as her departure was untimely.

It was the auspicious day of Hartalika Pujan—the day when all married women pay ritualistic obeisance to Goddess Hartalika and pray for their husbands' lifelong welfare and wellness. For Kantabai, every day was as auspicious as that one. However, why did she choose only that day for her final journey?

I will always remember that day vividly, just as I will remember her fondly forever. Her memories stir up many emotions in me. They sublimate me. And why should they not? It was a heartfelt, very intimate companionship of almost four and a half decades. The inseparable couple who loved each other more than themselves, were now separated.

Or were they? While embarking on this onward journey, everybody leaves everything behind. Everybody steps out empty handed. They leave behind their bodies and transmigrate just with their prana (soul). But she had left even her prana at my feet. Her heart ceased beating but her soul was left with me. So earnestly dedicated and self-effacing was 'She' to 'Me', who is known to the world as Bhavarlal Jain...

Really, 'She' and 'Me' is the only truth, as she had experienced it...

If anybody asks in future, 'Who was Kantabai?' first of all correct the use of tense. Then show him the direction of our home and our family. She lives on in our family's sanskaar. She exists in every atom of every family member—our four sons and their wives and their children. Not only in them, but she is subtly present in our entire extended family and thousands of associates of the socially conscious Jain business house.

And if anybody asks, 'Who was Bhavarlal Jain?' he may be told: He is the man who wrote the monograph *She and Me*, and through that 'He' made 'She' come alive forever. 'She' who symbolized the quintessence of Indian culture.

'He' was merely her husband.